The Holistic Health Nurse Series™
Eating4Eternity:

Unlock Your Holistic Health Lifestyle™

Jenny Berkeley, RN

Publisher:
CM BERKELEY MEDIA GROUP
Ontario, Canada
First Edition

Print Edition

Copyright © 2012 Jenny Berkeley
All rights reserved.

ISBN-13: 978-0-9868018-3-9

Look for more great titles from *The Holistic Health Nurse Series*™

www.holistichealthnurse.com

Selected Buyer Reviews

Not A Vegan, But Great Info! By Ryan (on Amazon)

Hello, I'm the world's biggest carnivore. I can't walk into a grocery store without pissing off the butchers. That's just how I am, I love meat, and without it I don't feel good. That being said, I'm concerned with staying healthy. Now I believe that meat is ESSENTIAL in a healthy diet, but I know many others that believe the exact opposite and seem to be pretty healthy. Different strokes for different blokes.

Even though this vegan/vegetarian minded, there was still a lot of great information about inner health. I like to pick up tidbits here and there by reading different things, and in my opinion, this was certainly worth the read. All-in-all, this was a winner, and if you're health conscious, or want to become health conscious, I recommend you take a look.

Perfect gift for your family by Mo Shine (on Amazon)

Having been an ardent reader of Jenny's magazine, Eternity Watch, for last one and half years, i was sure that this book was going to improvise my health habits and create a better understanding on medicines and ailments. And it did! I should thank Jenny for her style of writing- almost no jargon, nothing that barrier between you and the subject. With meal plans, tips and explanations i advice anyone who reads this book to keep a note book by their side to take down tips that matters to them. Jenny says in her book, "The influence of those closest to you can determine your health outcome in terms of the ability to help or hinder your efforts." so I suggest you to make your loved ones read this book as well. I gifted this book to my wife. After all, it is our family that determines our health! Happy reading!

This book will change lives! by Jean Hutchins (on Amazon)
This book is a well-thought-out plan for taking control of your own health and really turning your life around. The examples, insights, suggestions and tips are shared by a veteran nurse who realizes the strengths and weaknesses in both Western-centered and other medicines, diets, exercises and beliefs. Her wisdom shines through in a very relate-able, non-preachy and practical way. Plus it's just an enjoyable read! You will learn a great deal of information you've never considered, have a springboard for assessing your current thoughts and beliefs, and gain a workable plan for improving your overall health!

* * * * *

DEDICATION

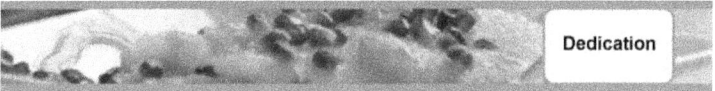

This book is dedicated to my dear husband
and loving children. They are the major
influences in my life and part of
what drives me to create
a healthier world.

* * * * *

ACKNOWLEDGMENTS

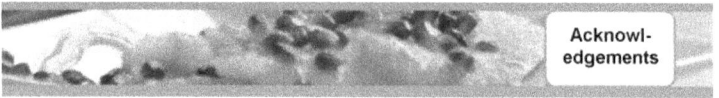

To produce a book these days takes the combined talents of a lot of people especially for a busy professional like myself. I have my different enterprises that I have to keep tabs on and so my time is so precious that it's sometimes takes real effort to get all the work done.

I do know that none of this would be possible without the help and assistance of all the people on my team. I want to acknowledge these people with love and gratitude in the universe.

Vaughn Berkeley, my business manager

Jean Hutchins, my editor

CM BERKELEY MEDIA GROUP, my publisher

Trusted Colleagues, my advanced readers

Thank you all.

* * * * *

CONTENTS

DEDICATION I
ACKNOWLEDGMENTS II
FOREWORD V
1 HEALTH ACCOUNTABILITY 7
2 THE NURSING ADVANTAGE 15
3 A NEW INCEPTION 19
4 LET THE DEAD BURY THEIR DEAD 29
5 LIVING FOODS FOR LIFEFORCE 36
6 CONVENIENCE VS. RIGHT 47
7 A PROGRAM THAT WORKS 54
8 KEEPING IT ON BUDGET 64
9 SAMPLE MEAL PLAN 69
10 A GLIMPSE OF THE FUTURE 92
MORE RESOURCES 97
ABOUT THE AUTHOR 98

Eating4Eternity - Unlock Your Holistic Health Lifestyle

FOREWORD

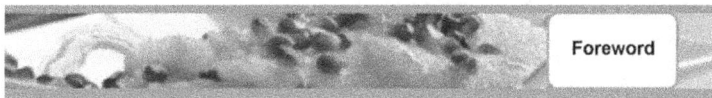

Having known Jenny for several years and having been a part of helping her with the realization of her dreams via the development of her website, Eating4Eternity.org and the creation and nurturing of her magazine, EternityWatch Magazine, I was delighted when asked to do the foreword to her book.

Jenny is a person who is truly passionate about health and wellness. The fact is, she honestly cares too much for her patients, her clients, and those around her. She cries when patients are crying, and she laughs when they are laughing. She is able to relate and connect with everyone involved in her care. This gift is one that few nurses and health professionals seem to possess today in the busy medical field.

Her passion is about educating people to live better lives. She believes that good health is everyone's birthright and that keeping it is a matter of personal choice. With that belief she has endeavoured to open up the lines of education to those who need it.

This book is perfectly aligned with her mission to educate people. In writing this book, her hope and passion was to share a part of herself with others and provide some sound advice. She wanted to act as a sort of early warning for some and a resource for others. I believe that she has managed to accomplish that with this book.

The book is short and well written for the newbie to the holistic health arena. She starts out by walking the reader through her insights into the medical field and by giving the reader a new understanding of health accountability and personal responsibility. She then builds on that concept by showing the reader how nurses are their best advocates within the industry that they will find themselves involved in one time or more in their lives.

Next, she gives the reader a new idea that transforms the mindset of the reader from the old-school mindset to the 21st century mindset for health. She unmasks some limiting beliefs and helps the reader discover their personal power through enlightenment.

Each succeeding chapter builds on a better understanding of the holistic health arena and Jenny takes a laddering approach in her delivery of the concepts. As the reader works through the book from chapter to chapter, the concepts build upon each other and take shape.

By the end of the book, there is only one choice left for the reader. That choice is to go boldly into a life that is focused on holistic health and wellness or meekly return to the path of pain, suffering and sorrow of an unenlightened life.

This was a thoroughly enjoyable read. It is a nice reading length to be able to deliver some fundamental concepts without having to spend days and days of reading. Jenny's style of writing is simple and non-technical, which is great for the average person.

I have no doubt that you will enjoy this book as much as I did.

Vaughn Berkeley, MBA
EternityWatch Magazine

* * * * *

1 HEALTH ACCOUNTABILITY

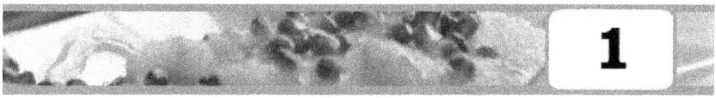

What do you think of when you think of health accountability? For some, it means that the doctors need to be more accountable for the treatments they use on patients. For others, it means that the hospitals need to be more accountable for the way they treat staff and patients. And for still others, it means a complete overhaul of the entire medical industry. But what does it mean to you?

Health accountability may indeed encompass elements of all of the above points depending on the perspective from which you choose to view the issue.

> I once heard that we each influence about 100 people at any given time in our lives. That may or may not be true, but you certainly do exercise some measure of influence over friends and family members. So taking responsibility for making sure that your influence in the realm of health and wellness is a positive one, is your choice and your duty.

Health accountability is everyone's responsibility. This should be your motto going forward if it is your choice to live all your later years in good health and wellness.

Of course, the medical industry needs to be fixed on a macro level. However, many of us are too far removed from the centers of power to create such a change. Also, there are numerous reports on the topic - by government, and regulatory committees, medical association committees and many other people - trying to work on the issue from that level.

We need change on a societal or community level. This type of change is one that is closer to your sphere of influence. I once heard that we each influence about 100 people at any given time in our lives. That may or may not be true, but you certainly do exercise some measure of influence over friends and family members. So taking responsibility for making sure that your influence in the realm of health and wellness is a positive one, is your choice and your duty.

The final level of influence in the realm of health accountability is the influence you hold over yourself. This is one area where you have almost absolute control and ability to create positive change.

However, I have found that it can be the very hardest for the individual to create meaningful and lasting change. Why? I suspect because you are too close to the issue and that sometimes gets in the way.

Let's recap the three spheres where health accountability is needed:
- The Macro Level (The Medical Industry)
- The Societal/Community Level
- The Individual Level

The subject of this book will not include looking at creating change on the Macro Level. This is because I am not part of the inner circle of decision makers with regards to the industry, nor do I seek such a position. I do have a high respect for those who take up those positions, but for me, it is too much time spent in meetings, developing policies that take a long time to implement, and all the while seeing patient experience remaining the same.

I'm a nurse and health educator and my personality is one that likes to stick closer to the grassroots level. I love being closer to the people and helping those who would help themselves.

The Societal/Community Level is one which I do enjoy. I hold lectures within the community on various aspects of health. Sometimes these lectures are free and other times they are for a fee. The purpose of these lectures is to educate people on the need for personal health accountability and responsibility.

As an adult, you alone are responsible for the choices you make that directly impact your current health and your future outlook. Sometimes there may be financial situations, social pressures, or other factors which influence your decisions, but ultimately you are the one making the decision.

I attempt to influence change by teaching others. But you can influence change by speaking to your friends, family members, and those you interact with at the club, or church, or local community center. The two ways you can help spread the message of health accountability is by talking to others about the concept and most importantly, being accountable, yourself.

This leads me to the third sphere of Individual Influence. Each day you are faced with thousands of decisions that impact the quality of your health. In fact, I see it in the hospital emergency departments where I work. I see the outcome of a series of poor choices that ultimately led to an unpleasant situation for the patient.

Could many of these have been avoided? In many cases, yes. Have you ever heard the saying that an ounce of prevention is worth a pound of cure. Well, that saying is as true today as it was decades ago, except with inflation; an ounce of prevention is probably worth about a kilogram of cure.

It is my purpose in this book to:
- Guide You to a Common-Sense Path to Health
- Show You the Pitfalls to Avoid
- Give You a Glimpse of the Coming Tsunami
- Show You an Easy Action Plan

Is this book for everyone? Absolutely, it is for everyone. It is for the patients I see who end up becoming regulars in the emergency room. It is for the doctors and nurses who are suffering from the same ailments that their patients are seeking help for. It is for the skeptical and those already on the path to health and wellness enlightenment. This book is for you.

I am not the kind of person to be long-winded about anything. And you will find that my book has very little excipients or fillers. I tend to stick to the point, build on it, give some strategies for doing it and then I move on to the next point.

So looking at health accountability, we can see in table 1 an overview of the type and the effort level.

Table 1: Health Accountability Type and Effort

Health Accountability Type	Change Effort Level
Macro (Medical Industry)	Very Hard
Society/Community	Medium
Individual	Easy

We can now understand that the greatest change in the shortest possible time will not come from the macro level. I see people on the news constantly complaining about the health care system both in Canada and in the United States. People can complain until they are blue in the face. Systemic change on a macro level takes an enormous amount of time. It can be compared to the movement of a glacier.

If you are someone with a sickness, you can't wait for the health industry to change in order to get the results you want. You have to change to get the result you want.

Do you want a life of good health, strength, and vitality?

Did you answer yes? I'm sure you did. In fact, if you ask anyone on the planet if they want good health, strength and vitality, I'm certain that all of them would say yes, they wanted it. So you are part of the normal group of people around the world who desire health.

What stops them and many others from having the life of good health they desire is that they have stopped holding themselves accountable for their health and well-being.

I am telling you that good health, strength and vitality requires change. Human beings, as well as most living things, require change to maintain vigor and vitality.

Think of a fish in a fish bowl. If you never changed the water, would that fish continue to live in health and vitality? Of course not. The fish would eventually die from its world becoming stagnant. How about another example? What if the world did not turn on its regular rotation, but stopped? Half of the earth would experience too much heat and the other half would experience too much cold. This would create an extremely unpleasant living environment.

> **Using the space below or a separate sheet of paper, write all the reasons you want to have more health, strength and vitality.**

Like the fish bowl or the rotating earth, change is built into your very existence. If I told you that you are changing whether you are aware of it or not, but you can positively control the flow of change to your benefit, would you like to know more?

Thank you for taking the time to complete that short exercise. It is important for you to understand the reasons you want more health.

Have you ever seen a child who wanted a toy of some kind so badly? Have you also seen that child who wanted that toy throw it away after only a short period of use? Without understanding why you want health, you will act as that child with the new toy. You will enjoy your health for a short time, but will toss it aside shortly.

If you didn't do the exercise or skipped it, maybe now is a good time to go back to completing it. Don't worry, the book will be here when you get back.

When did society begin losing its health accountability?

It began when individuals in society began placing their responsibility in the hands of others. When you decide to give up your responsibility and place it in another's hands, then you are losing personal responsibility. And this is precisely what happened in the turn of the last century.

Consider that prior to 1900 most people ate locally from what was grown around them. Food from this source was inspected by each person before they consumed it. The person was responsible for harvesting it at the right time, separating the good from the spoiled produce, cleaning and preparing it properly, and then eating it.

Around the 1920s a new thing came on the market, called supplements. People could suddenly choose to get their "nutrients" from a pill or oil instead of the whole food source. In the 1940s "Recommended Daily Allowances" came into being and now people could be told the minimum amount of food they could eat to avoid getting sick. I think of the recommended daily allowance as the least amount of "nutrition" I should consume to avoid getting sick. Then, when possible, I eat a bit more than the RDA level.

My objective is not to eat enough to avoid sickness, but to eat enough to facilitate vitality.

By the 1950s and 60s, convenience was the most desired trait for foods. TV dinners, heavily processed canned foods, and juices, with loads of chemical preservatives and processing became the norm. Again, society gave up its responsibility of ensuring that the quality of the food consumed was good for the body.

This is just a small example of where things started to go wrong.

But this book is not about just blaming the past. It is about taking the higher path - going forward into the future; your future.

Summary of Chapter 1

In this chapter, we looked at the term health accountability and what it means to your personal health and wellness outcomes.

We discussed that complaining and waiting on the medical system to fix its numerous shortcomings is not going to help your immediate health situation.

We look at where things went wrong and just how history has seen people give up their personal responsibility and accountability to themselves.

* * * * *

2 THE NURSING ADVANTAGE

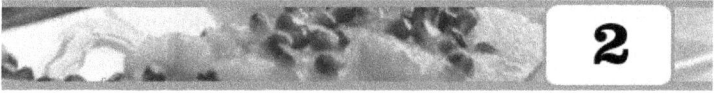

Nurses are really the best advocates that patients have in the medical system. Doctors are the professionals, but how much face-time do patients really get with a doctor these days - five or ten minutes? Nurses are the ones who interact with patients on an ongoing basis during their stay in the hospital.

Nurses have a very special position in the medical industry. They support the medical infrastructure. Consider a nurse working in an emergency room (ER) of a hospital. There may be 5 ER doctors and each of them is an expert in five medications. That's 25 medications in total for simplicity sake.

Now a nurse during the course of time, will become an expert in each of those 25 medications because it is the nurse who is responsible for administering the dosages, reviewing the contraindications, and studying the side effects of the medication.

I have been a nurse both locally in Canada and abroad. In my observations of nursing and nurses, I can certainly say that it takes a special kind of caring person to take up the position of a nurse. It takes an even better person to last any period of time in that profession. Having been a nurse for over 20 years now, I have seen all type of nurses, patients, doctors and have also observed their interactions with each other.

Nurses are the ones who can bring about the greatest change in the lives of the individual as well as the medical professional. However, nurses need to be educated on the holistic approach to health and wellness in order for that change to begin.

In publishing my magazine, EternityWatch Magazine, on health and wellness, I have found nurses to be a great source of assistance. Don't get me wrong. It's not all sunshine and roses, but for the most part, nurses want to see things improve for the patients because they develop a greater connection with each patient.

Nurses develop this connection because they end up spending more time with the patient during their hospital stay or their stay at a private clinic. This time allows for relationship building, which can add value to the healing process.

But not all nurses are progressive, or even suited to the job. Some chose the profession for financial gain or job security instead of for the purpose of helping the sick. And so, some of those people have a crabby attitude. There are other nurses who are sick because they, themselves are not aware of the principles of holistic health and wellness.

Then there are the ones who are sick and tired of the profession and are on the way to being burned out. I remember one time speaking with a young nurse. She was only a couple of years in the profession but she was constantly swearing under her tongue.

When I had a conversation with her, I noted that she had only been a nurse for a couple of years. She told me that she was sick of this job,

> I can honestly say that being a nurse has been the best experience of my life. It has allowed me to positively impact the lives of thousands of people who came into the hospital during my two decades

dealing with the never-ending flow of sick and aged people. She was ready to quit her job. I began to wonder what would happen if many more young nurses decided to leave the profession early. This could be a potentially catastrophic phenomenon in the medical profession because there is a huge need for nurses.

I can honestly say that being a nurse has been the best experience of my life. It has allowed me to positively impact the lives of thousands of people who came into the hospital during my two decades.

There are times when I cried with the patients and their family members. There are times in which I laughed with the patients and their family members. I have also been an advocate for patients when they needed me to be. And I have also been a source and a resource for doctors when they needed my input.

Many a fresh young graduate doctor has taken some advice from this old war horse.

But nursing alone is not enough. There must be more. The profession is too narrow in the way it teaches the curriculum. It needs to expand to focus on various aspects of nutrition and the linkages between holistic living and health.

At one point in my life, years ago I faced my own personal medical trauma. I was suffering from a mysterious pain in my stomach that the doctors could not explain. My tests came back fine but I was facing pain whenever I ate food. I remember one time driving to work in pain, hoping and praying that I did not have stomach cancer.

A series of events in my life would, by divine arrangement, lead me to the path to health and wellness.

Once I started on that path, I was completely cured of that mystery pain. And it has never returned.

I place a greater value on my health and wellness now more than ever. And now that I am fully mindful of the holistic approach we need to have in life, I put it into practice in my personal life and with my clients.

Nursing has been a wonderful advantage in my life because it has also enabled me to see what is coming down the medical pipeline. I can with some certainty, foresee how the medical industry will take shape in the next 10 to 20 years. Let me tell you that if you do not take the time to take responsibility for your health now, it will be too late in the next 5, 10 or 20 years.

Summary of Chapter 2

In this chapter, we looked at the key role the nursing profession has in the continuity of patient care.

We also looked at some of the ways the nursing profession is under pressure and where there are areas to improve.

I also shared how the profession has been the best place for me personally.

* * * * *

3 A NEW INCEPTION

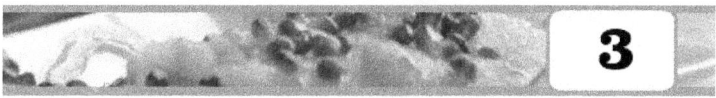

Oftentimes you will hear me talk about the need for a new thinking around health and wellness for the consumer. Think about this logically for a moment. The definition of insanity is doing the same thing over and over and trying to get a different result each time.

Now suppose you have been doing the same thing in your life for the past five, ten or twenty years? The person you are now, is the result of doing that. Do you suppose that if you continue as you have been doing all along that you will now get a different result?

The simple answer to that question is no. You will not get a different result. And to add insult to injury, each day you spend doing the wrong thing is one day less that you have to do the right thing. You lose both ways.

> ...each day you spend doing the wrong thing is one day less that you have to do the right thing. You lose both ways.

What is needed is a new way of thinking and a new method to address the issues in your life. But a new idea is not always accepted. And your mind may offer a lot of resistance to your new ideas. Sometimes where your mind leaves off, your friends and family will pick up offering resistance to your new ideas.

Ultimately, only you can live your life and you reap the benefits or the losses of what you plant. Everyone else can only offer cheap talk.

Ask yourself this question:

What could possibly be wrong with some of the things in my life that may be causing me to become sick? (Write your answers in the space below or on a sheet of paper.)

Now ask yourself this question:

How ready am I to give up the things that I wrote earlier? (Write your answers in the space below or on a sheet of paper.)

If you are at a point in your life where you are not willing to give up the items that may be making you sick, then don't beat yourself up.

The timing is just not right for you. Maybe there is something there that simply is not clicking. If that is the case, then why not sleep on the issue? A good night's rest may be exactly what you need to help put things into perspective.

Now we'll look at some of the limiting beliefs that may have been shaping your existence up until now.

Limiting Belief #1: What I eat does not have any major impact on my health, strength, and vitality.

This is a very strong belief to fight against because it was most likely coded into your mind when you were a child. And as a child, there was little to no resistance to your programming. Everything was recorded as the ultimate truth; thus, as an adult it takes mindful effort to change that belief.

It is not impossible. There are thousands of people who make the transition every day around the globe. But there are also people who fail to achieve that mental mind shift.

Now you may be thinking that you were never the kind of person to believe that what you eat does not affect your health. However, the litmus test is in your own health.

Are you a sickly person? Did you suddenly come down with some catastrophic disease? If your answer is yes to either of those questions then you have been defined by that limiting belief #1.

Limiting Belief #2: Hospitals are the best place for you in the world when you are sick.

This is a very strong belief to fight against because it is constantly ingrained in the minds of everyone on a regular basis. Television shows make hospitals seem like sexy and glamorous places to be. The doctors and nurses look like angels instead of like ordinary people.

But the reality is that the hospital can be a dangerous place to the health of individuals. Now I am NOT saying abolish hospitals. Hospitals serve a very important function in society as treatment facilities for patients with certain types of conditions.

According to the World Health Organization (WHO), in a report released the week of July 25, 2011, "Millions of people die each year from medical errors and infections linked to health care and going into the hospital is far riskier than flying."

According to the WHO, if you were admitted to the hospital in any country in the world, your chances of experiencing a medical error would be 1 in 10. Your chances of dying would be 1 in 300 due to the error.

Why does the WHO give such a warning about hospitals? Well, in one of my blog posts in early 2011, I noted some doctors protesting at a hospital in Quebec, Canada. These ER physicians had enough of the state of their work environment. On the YouTube video, you see the French doctors give a walkthrough of the ER. You can see torn beds where possible contamination of patients can occur. You see mold from the ceiling vents. You see the toilet being used as a coat hanger. And you see an infectious disease isolation room that is nothing more than a curtain pulled around the patient.

All of those things add up to a hospital environment that is a breeding ground for germs. This is the major risk to patients when they go into hospital. If a sick person with an already weakened immune system goes to the hospital and stays for any length of time, they become exposed to the numerous germs left by others and circulating in the air, on door handles, on the floors, and everywhere else.

Sometimes, depending on the type of issue you are dealing with, a family physician, or small local clinic may be the best place to get treatment. Perhaps going to a naturopathic doctor may be another good option.

Do you automatically think of running to the hospital when you have some kind of illness? If so, then you may be operating under limiting belief #2.

Limiting Belief #3: Nothing is visibly wrong with me, so there is no need to change anything.

This is taking the "if it ain't broke, don't fix it" philosophy a bit too far. From the moment we come forth from the womb, we begin dying. Our cells are continuously aging. You should understand that the body is wonderfully adaptive, so that you rarely ever feel the burden of your choices up front.

This means that at some later date the effects of a lifetime of poor choices will catch up to you. Even if you think there is nothing wrong, there may be something brewing inside your body.

Have you ever heard anyone say they were fit as a fiddle, then suddenly they got a heart attack (at age 45)? Or have you heard of people who were seemingly okay and went in for a checkup only to discover later that they have full-blown stage 4 cancer?

These ailments do not just show up overnight. They are not like fancy sports cars that go from zero to 100 in seconds. These diseases grow slowly in the body. This is because each day the body is resisting the growth of the disease. It is when the battle is lost on one day that the disease grows a little more.

Because many people are insensitive to the workings of their bodies, they misunderstand warning signs. They take pills to suppress the symptoms and eventually get the bad news.

But sometimes people are aware, and they can tell something is not quite right with their bodies. They cannot put their finger on it but they know that there is a problem.

This is the consciousness awakening within the patient's body. You should embrace it and work with your doctor to figure out what is going wrong. Modern science has wonderful diagnostic tools and reports to help you figure out the symptoms.

Limiting Belief #4: If I ignore it, it will just go away.

This limiting belief is as dangerous as the previous one. In this mindset, the patient is aware of the problem but has decided to ignore it.

There are many reasons for ignoring a problem within the body. One reason could be fear. A person could be very afraid of the result of any tests, so they choose to not do them. They have the incorrect belief that no news is good news. But when something is going wrong in the body, a living machine, no news is not good news at all.

The other reason people may ignore a problem is lack of money. In places where people have to pay for basic health care, you may find that people put off visiting the doctor, dentist, or optician because they need to use that money elsewhere. Thankfully in Canada we have universal access to basic health services. However, people in countries where you have to pay for health care MUST develop within themselves a fundamental understanding of health and wellness principles so that they can address minor things themselves.

Limiting Belief #5: There is no difference between living food and dead food; between whole food supplements and synthetic supplements; between organic foods and conventional.

This limiting belief is also dangerous and very much a path which removes you from the true path to health and wellness. Whenever you encounter such a limiting belief, then consider the litmus test. Take a raw, uncooked, living seed and one which you cooked. Place both of them in the ground. If there is truly no difference, then they will both grow. However we know that they will not both grow. The cooked seed will rot and decompose in the soil while the uncooked seed will grow into a plant.

This unexplainable life-force is one of nature's most powerful examples that life is more than what science can understand.

Likewise, there is a difference between whole food supplements made from the entire plant and its constituent components and a synthetic supplement made in a laboratory. While science may not fully comprehend the difference, the body which is intelligently designed, knows the difference.

Limiting Belief #6: If it is not conventional medicine, then it must be quackery.

Conventional medicine is characterized by diagnostic machinery, prescription drugs, surgery, and hospitals. People are used to this today, but in the late 1800s and early 1900s the conventional medical doctor was a poor professional.

During those days, it was the holistic healer who was of greater importance and whose medical expertise was more sought after. And so a war began to brew between the naturopaths (holistic medicine) and the allopaths (conventional medicine).

The deciding factor was the alliance made between big business and the conventional medicine industry. Big business saw that conventional medicine treatments, diagnostic devices, and other supporting items could be quite profitable to the industry.

Money and power managed to influence academia where allopathic medicine was able to win the position of influence. Thus holistic medicine would take considerable blows. However, it was not ever to be counted out. This is because people exist as a whole entity, not in parts. Treatments which neglect the whole will undoubtedly do unintentional harm elsewhere while attempting to fix one area. Hence the growing list of side effects for certain drugs.

Today the science is behind the need to take medicine to the holistic field. And it is there that many people are experiencing healing without the dangerous side effects.

If one follows strictly the belief that conventional medicine is the only way, then a person would limit their options in seeking their personal health and wellness.

Traditional Chinese Medicine (TCM) is based on Eastern and Oriental teachings on healing the body. This is based on thousands of years of history and should be considered as a valuable tool in your health and wellness toolkit.

Chiropractic medicine is another very valuable resource in seeking healing. Did you know that just a couple of decades ago, insurance companies refused to cover chiropractic treatment because they were skeptical of its effectiveness? Today chiropractic treatments are covered and it does work.

Massage and physiotherapy are other options that help the body to unwind and place itself in a healing mode. These should not be discounted.

If you find your mind closed to the possibility of a naturopathic doctor, chiropractor, or other holistic healer, then you may be experiencing limiting belief #6.

Summary of Chapter 3

In this chapter, we looked at six limiting beliefs that shape the way people perceive health and wellness. These six limiting beliefs combined in a single mindset is enough to resign that person to a life sentence of ill health.

The six limiting beliefs covered are:
- **#1: What I eat does not have any major impact on my health, strength, and vitality.**
- **#2: Hospitals are the best place for you in the world when you are sick.**

- #3: Nothing is visibly wrong with me, so there is no need to change anything.
- #4: If I ignore it, it will just go away.
- #5: There is no difference between living food and dead food; between whole food supplements and synthetic supplements; between organic foods and conventional.
- #6: If it is not conventional medicine, then it must be quackery.

*****.

4 LET THE DEAD BURY THEIR DEAD

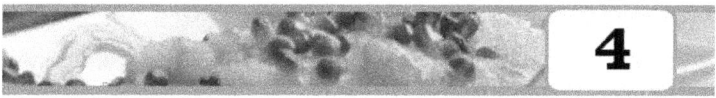

This chapter is one that takes a higher-level look at the human condition and the linkage to sickness, disease, and death. The chapter title, "Let the dead bury the dead," is a title that is taken from ancient writing and seems a bit paradoxical. A person can ask, "How can the dead bury themselves?"

On the physical level of our understanding, we know that the dead cannot bury themselves, but it is the living who bury the dead. So what is the significance of this saying?

Let me give you the spiritual context of this saying before I tell you how I have used it in the medical sense.

Jesus the Christ was just retiring from a long day of healing. By the evening, word had spread that the healer was in town and people came from all over with their sicknesses to be healed. Finally the crowd seemed to be growing and growing, so Jesus the Christ gave the command to depart to the other side. One of the disciples said to Jesus that he would follow him anywhere but first he needed to go home to bury his dead father. But Jesus the Christ, answered him, "Follow me; and let the dead bury their dead."

From the story, we can see illustrated here that Christ appears to be telling his disciple to let the other dead people bury the dead. Christ was a spiritual teacher and was considered the light of the world. Those in darkness and in death therefore are supposed to bury their dead. Jesus the Christ, being the light and the life, wanted his disciples to focus on his spiritual ministry.

How is this story even practical to the medical mission of this book to educate you on health and wellness?

It speaks to a person's personal mindset. If a person's mind is made up that there is nothing beside pills that can help them, then by their own mind, they have condemned themselves to a life of sickness and death. Life, or rather, the hope of life is not in them.

As a person reading this book, I do not consider you a "dead." Your very act of seeking knowledge of health and wellness draws you to the living side. A sincere quest will bring people and knowledge into your life that will help you find the path to personal healing, health and wellness.

The mind, then, is the focus of this chapter. I once heard a television pastor tell a story about a man who was deathly afraid of being locked in a refrigerator car of a train. He was a repair man and this was his personal nightmare. He was afraid of being locked inside the car and being frozen to death.

It happened that one weekend while working on a box-car, he got locked in. When the man's body was discovered after the weekend, he appeared to have died from exposure to freezing cold. On the floor, written in his blood were the words, "So Cold." The amazing thing was that the refrigerator box-car was not functional.

There was no way the man could have died from freezing cold. Yet the man's body had exhibited all the signs of hypothermia, and death from freezing cold. He in essence, died from a fictional disease made real by the infinite power of his mind.

And this unfortunately, is the situation of too many people in society today. They are suffering from a disease which they could very easily overcome, but their mind has given the disease more power over them. Their mind has amplified the force of the disease.

It's a bit like the Bart Simpson cartoon where he doesn't want to go to school. He begins to think that he wants to be sick. Then you see his immune-system cells talking. They are like a little army. The commanding officer tells the troops that they are receiving orders from command to surrender. The commanding officer says to the soldier, that it must be a school day. Then he tells the other immune-system cells to surrender. It is funny when we see it in a cartoon, but there is an amazing amount of truth hidden in that short cartoon scenario.

The mind can influence your healing. It can hinder it or help it. If you believe that you will not get better, then nothing short of God himself descending from the sky to heal you will help you get well. This is because you have positioned your entire being to suffer with sickness.

At Hippocrates Health Institute in Florida I have heard a funny saying. If you've been doing the raw foods, the cleansing, the detox, the supplements, the complete program, and you are still not getting better, then the problem was not there. The problem is either your job, your family members, your friends, or even your spouse/partner.

And this leads us back to "Let the dead bury their dead." When you begin to put your mind into the path of healing and holistic practices, if those closest to you are totally against it, then you need to separate yourself from them. Because they (their minds) are dead to holistic health, and they want to bury their dead (you when you die).

It might sound rough, but sometimes it is a necessary truth you need to understand. The influence of those closest to you can determine your health outcome in terms of the ability to help or hinder your efforts.

Sometimes when you are going through a traumatic sickness, you will need to make new friends who desire to live life with all of their being. When you are in a battle against a disease, you need three things.

Firstly, you need experienced commanding officers who can help you negotiate the terrain of your battle. These are the holistic health professionals, the naturopathic doctors, the chiropractors, the traditional Chinese medicine practitioners, the holistic nurses like me. We are your coaches, guides, support.

Secondly, you need family members who support you 100 percent. You don't need them second-guessing you, questioning you at every turn, making you afraid and doubtful, or scaring you to death. Family members with such negative energies around you are not beneficial. If you have ten family members where eight are negative and two are positive, send the eight home and just keep the two. They will be more beneficial to you than the other eight.

It might seem corny or cliché, but it is so very important where your health and well-being is concerned. If you have ever spent time in a hospital as a patient or a medical professional, did you ever notice that patients who are surrounded by loving family members seem to do a little better or have a more positive attitude than the ones without family members around?

Having someone who cares, makes a whole world of difference. However, there is a difference between caring to the point of stifling your health and wellness options and caring enough to allow you to choose the path to health and wellness that is right for you.

The person who is close to you does not need to necessarily be a relative. Sometimes a family doctor can be the one closing your opportunities to health and wellness. For example, one author and lecturer I know speaks of his personal experience with IBD or Crohn's Disease. He tells of the time when he asked his doctor if he should eat raw foods and she told him definitely not. So he did it anyway and began to experience some relief.

He also jokes that at some point, whenever he asked her about something, the more she was against it, the more he would be willing to try it. He healed himself of IBD when he was told it was incurable.

Note that I am not suggesting you disregard the advice of a trained medical doctor. What I am suggesting, is that you exercise a bit of product comparison. There are numerous doctors of different degrees of knowledge. Some of them just barely passed the medical exams to become a doctor while others were A+ medical students. Some keep learning and growing in their knowledge while others refuse to learn and be open minded.

The open minded, A+ doctors are the ones you want to seek out. So if one doctor gives you one opinion and it does not satisfy you, seek out other doctors and get their opinions. Find one who is knowledgeable in holistic health and conventional medicine. Such a doctor truly understands how the body works, how disease works, and how to get to the root of the problem, not just the symptom. They are doctors of the living.

Today, you can Google-search doctors to see if they have published any papers or reports or articles. You can get a sense of where their thinking is. If you can't find any published information from your doctor or the doctor you are thinking of seeing, then they are most likely not very innovative.

Thirdly, you need the strength of will to move forward with your chosen path. You are your own best asset in your healing. You are both the foundation and the structure of your future. All of your future will be based on your present choices. You are so much in control that it is truly empowering once you understand it.

Knowing that you are created to have dominion over sickness and disease and to be able to live a life of health, joy and abundance, must cause you to double or triple your efforts to strengthen your mind and your spirit, and then your body will follow.

Love yourself first of all. If no one in the world has loved you, you must begin by loving yourself. Your good parts and bad parts. Life may have been a struggle, but as long as you are alive, life is yours.

Don't hang around with negative people whose only contribution to your well-being is doom and gloom. They are rain clouds that hide your sunshine, but you can avoid them or drive them away. It is in your best interest when you are seeking wellness.

Let the dead bury their dead. You are a member of the living and you will hold on to life for all its worth with every fibre of your being.

Summary of Chapter 4

There are two kinds of people on the planet. They are called the living, and, the dead. They have two very different approaches to health, well-being, vitality, and living in harmony with the planet.

In this chapter, we looked at how you can associate with the right people to help you accelerate your health and wellness journey. Start by finding qualified and mindful health professionals. Next, we talked about keeping family members and those with open minds close to you as you explore your options. Even your family doctor should come under scrutiny if their mind is closed. Finally, we touched on you being your own natural resource in your path to healing. Nurture yourself, care for yourself, and love yourself on the path.

* * * * *

5 LIVING FOODS FOR LIFEFORCE

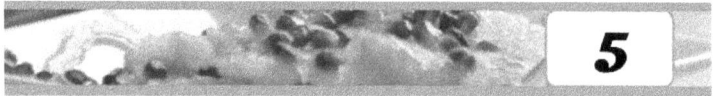

Food is an essential ingredient in life. It is important for all living organisms on this planet. Humans are the only creatures that cook their foods before eating them. In order to transform your life, you need to look at the life in your food. We are, after all, living beings and we should consume what continues to feed our life energy.

The Difference Between Living and Dead Food

Food is an essential part of who we are. The saying that "we are what we eat (and drink)" is as true now as it ever was. The Raw Food movement is about attempting to eat foods that are uncooked and therefore still have all of their vital elements intact.

Cooked food is considered dead food. Whether your food is steamed, broiled, fried, or baked, it is considered cooked and dead. Why do we consider it dead food? Because all of the life force contained within the food has been destroyed by the cooking process. And we always go back to the litmus test on the matter.

Cook a seed and take a raw, uncooked seed. Plant them both into the soil and see if both will grow. Of course, only the raw seed will grow. This is because the life is still in it, whereas the life has been destroyed in the cooked seed.

If cooked food is the thesis, then raw food is the antithesis. The raw food movement is about eating foods raw. In some cases, foods are "cooked" or rather dehydrated at a low temperature so that the moisture is removed without killing any of the enzymes, nutrients or other life-force elements.

What is it about cooked food that makes it not the best raw materials for the human body?

Cooking involves heating food to a high temperature. This temperature destroys vital enzymes contained within the food. Where there are proteins or amino acids, they become coagulated and therefore more difficult for the body to assimilate. Vitamins are also destroyed from cooking by morphing into forms that are again, difficult for the body to use. Toxins such as herbicides, fungicides, and pesticides have their toxicity further enhanced in the cooking process. Oxygen is heated out of the food, leaving it in a deoxygenated state for the body to try to absorb.

While all of this is happening to the cooked food, you must remember that this is even before the food hits your lips. All this deforming, denaturing, and degradation of the food is taking place in your cooking pot, or microwave, or baking dish.

If you could take a high-powered microscope and see the stuff left behind for your body to consume, you would be disgusted at what you saw. Especially if you compared that image with the image of the same food in its raw, uncooked state.

Cooked food also causes a pathogenic response in the body. This reaction, called leukocytosis, is where the white blood cells of the body are used to break down the cooked food, similar to the way they attack foreign invaders to the body. Scientists believed this was a normal reaction at first, but Dr. Paul Kouchakoff, M.D. proved otherwise in 1930 when he demonstrated that eating raw foods does not produce the same leukocytosis response within the body.

The conclusion to be drawn from this was that something in the cooked food triggered (or perhaps the cooked food itself triggered) an autoimmune response within the body that was not triggered by the raw foods.

We need a healthy and active immune system which is focused on killing unwanted germs within our bodies. Does it make sense to you to have to divide those precious resources so that they are busy with food when they should be fighting other germs? If eating raw foods allows your body to focus 95 to 100% of your white blood cells on your disease, then it's a simple thing. Eat raw foods to ease or remove the burden on your immune system. Then it can focus on killing your disease and healing your body.

So, Why Do We Love Cooked Food?

When we are born, we don't start out loving cooked foods. Breast milk is not boiled first before it is given to infants. And everyone knows that mother's milk is still the best source of living foods and nutrients for a baby.

Observe toddlers when they are first being introduced to cooked foods. When you put the food in their mouths, they spit it out. You try again and they spit again. You practically have to force-feed them that first cooked meal.

They continue to resist the cooked food until their bodies finally adapt to it and they stop fighting you. At this point they are eating it on their own. Their minds and bodies have now been successfully programmed to like the cooked food.

So why do we, as adults, love cooked foods? One reason is because we are programmed to love it from a very young age. We are exposed to cooked foods that our parents eat. And so, without being able to resist it and not having free choice at that age, we as children, develop an attachment to cooked food.

As we get older, we begin to associate emotions to cooked and processed foods that further cement our attachment to those foods. Candies are used to bribe children to behave or as rewards for desired behaviours. So children develop an attachment early on to sweets. Many cooked dishes are also used as comfort foods when a child is upset or uncomfortable. So the child develops an emotional link between food and comfort.

By the time you get to adulthood, it all seems so natural to feel the way you do about your cooked food. And this natural behaviour is what brings you the most comfort in your world. The surety that you can turn to chocolate for comfort, for example, or that a nice bowl of your favourite soup is ready and waiting can have a large psychological impact.

When you are stressed out and need some sense of comfort, it is amazing how quickly a person turns to food as a source of comfort. And this is why you and the world are hooked on the cook.

What About Animal Foods?

According to the dictionary, a corpse is a "dead body." If you see a dead animal on the side of the highway do you think of it as food? Do you pull your car over and get a bag to take home the free food? Of course not.

There is something about a dead animal on the side of the road that makes your mind and stomach shout, "No way... I'm not eating that!"

But when you go to the shelves in your big box supermarket, your mouth begins to salivate at the thought of preparing that red and tender-looking corpse. My uncle-in-law has said, that in the islands, the Rastas say that "their chest is not a graveyard so they're not burying (eating) any corpse (dead animals)." (emphasis added) There is some wisdom in that dietary choice.

All flesh decomposes. That is a fact of life. The meat on the shelves appears to be red and juicy, fresh and tender, because of the chemical treatments it has undergone. It has been injected with chemicals to enhance redness of the flesh. The flesh of a dead animal a few days old would already look grey and discoloured. The animal meats have been treated with chemicals to kill the microbes that would have already begun decomposing the flesh, causing it to rot.

If beauty is only skin deep, then the butchers and meat processors have found a way to take it beyond, to the flesh and bone, using chemicals. Because if you saw the true nature of that rotting flesh, you would not be keen to buy it. No one would want to buy it because it would remind you of the dead animal on the side of the road.

If cooked plant foods created an autoimmune response in the digestive system, do you think that cooked meats would create a similar response?

Absolutely, yes. In fact, the cooked meats would begin to rot a lot sooner than the cooked plant materials, thereby creating a need for a much higher immune system response in the gut to fight off the toxins created as a result.

So you have to decide where you want your white blood cells to focus their attention. Do you want them fighting your infection, disease or cancer? Or do you want them fighting the toxins contained in your rotting meats and other cooked foods?

Your internal resources are limited, so you have to choose in which area you want your biological defences deployed. For me personally, if I was sick in hospital, I'd avoid the cooked food and work with someone to provide me with fresh raw, organically prepared dishes that do not add to my body's burden and also strengthen my immune system to fight my illness.

Why Choose A Raw Food Diet?

A Raw Food Diet is one which has all of the following intact:
- Live Enzymes
- Whole, Intact Vitamins and Minerals
- Whole Food Nutrients
- Cellular Oxygen
- The Life Force Not Diminished

Let's take a look at each of the points mentioned earlier with respect to their presence in the raw food.

The live enzymes of the food are important in the digestion of the food. All plant foods contain within them, the enzymes necessary for breaking them down into their basic components. If you want to use this analogy to visualise the meaning, you can think of a combination lock.

Your food is a combination lock with the combination keys right on the lock. The enzymes contained within the food is the correct combination that will unlock your food's nutrients for your body. When you cook the food, it is like destroying the combination keys on the lock. Now the only way to open that lock is by a brute-force attack.

> Your food is a combination lock with the combination keys right on the lock. The enzymes contained within the food is the correct combination that will unlock your food's nutrients for your body. When you cook the food, it is like destroying the combination keys on the lock. Now the only way to open that lock is by a brute-force attack.

With your food, when it is cooked, you have to apply brute force to digest it. This brute force is your stomach, your immune system, white blood cells, and your own digestive enzymes.

With your raw foods, you have the combination intact, and the lock works fine. Your stomach is able to turn it up and the lock unlocks easily, releasing your food's nutrients into your digestive tract. Little or no white blood cells are required and a drastically reduced amount of your own digestive enzymes are utilized in the process.

Your body then has the raw foods with the enzymes intact for your health and well-being without the added baggage of increased body burden.

Having your raw food with its whole, intact vitamins and minerals means that your body will have the vitamins and minerals it needs in a readily absorbable form. These vitamins and minerals have the value in your body of helping your body to maintain balance in pH levels, in building up bones and organs, and in overall maintenance of the body.

Whole food nutrients are another essential component of a raw food diet. These whole food nutrients, such as phyto-nutrients, are not vitamins and minerals, but are nutrients produced within the plant and which work within your body to help create optimum health. Science is beginning to understand how these phyto-nutrients work, but there is so much more to be learned about them in nature. One thing we do know is that they are essential to the body in helping maintain health, wellness, and vitality.

Cellular oxygen is another component of your raw foods. You want your food to be raw because it contains its own supply of oxygen. Cooking the food removes any oxygen that was contained within it. This cellular oxygen helps in the digestion and assimilation of the nutrients and also passes oxygen into your digestive tract. You need this fibre and cellular oxygen intact within your raw food.

The life force of the food must not be diminished when you are using a raw foods diet. All living things die. When we eat a raw food diet, we are trying to preserve the food's living status as much as possible before we consume it.

Foods picked fresh from your garden or from your local farmer are ideal for the amount of life-force energy contained within the food. Sprouts are also another excellent source of living foods.

Raw Foods vs. Living Foods

At this point, now is a good opportunity to make a finer distinction between raw foods and living foods. At one end of the spectrum of eating, you have people who eat mostly cooked foods and processed foods. Their bodies are paying the price day after day and year after year.

In an effort to combat that, you have the concept of raw foods. A commitment to a raw-foods diet allows the individual to begin putting back more raw foods into their system as well as taking out the processed and cooked foods. It is a great transition stage. Raw foods should be raw, ripe, fresh, and organic. They should consist of seeds, grains, nuts, fruits, and vegetables and green leafy vegetables.

As a person begins to make the effort to eat more raw and wholesome foods, their programming towards foods becomes altered. Also, many of the emotions associated with food get reassessed. It can be a truly life-changing process.

Once you are eating more or mostly raw, the finer distinction is in how alive your food is. By that I mean, was that plum picked green in some third world country and traveling three weeks on a boat before arriving in Canada or your country? Has the food in essence, been dying for three weeks prior to your coming along to buy it and then eat it?

The answer to that question makes all the difference in the world. It is like the dead animal on the side of the road imagery we used earlier. If your produce has been dying since it was picked weeks back, plus it spent extra time on the store shelves before you bought it and took it home, then the life-force of that food has been slipping away all the time.

Ideally you would have your own garden where your transit-time from your food source to your mouth is minutes. You're getting it as alive as you can.

The next best thing is from your local farmer. I visit the farmer's markets and often chat with the farmers while I buy their produce. Many of them will harvest their product in the morning to sell it in the market in the afternoon. In this case, the transit time could be hours. If you put some of the items in your fridge, then that transit time becomes days.

This is why it is important to eat local and support your local farmers. They are actually helping you gain access to the life force of the foods you eat when you buy from them.

The one sort of exception in this is seeds. Seeds can last for months, years or decades in the correct environment. Once your seeds are sprouted, then they must be eaten within a relatively short period of time. They are your sprouts and they are bursting with life energy, nutrients, and all the goodness your body requires.

Sprouts are also a good supplement to your diet in the winter time when farm-fresh food is not readily available. When you don't have access to the foods you regularly purchase from your local farmer, then get out those sprouting jars or your special sprouter and begin growing your own microgreens to eat.

When you have reached a point where your diet consists of living foods and not just raw foods, then you are on a higher path of dietary consciousness.

Your health and well-being is important, so do what you can with the knowledge you have.

Summary of Chapter 5

In this chapter, we looked at the fundamental differences in a living-dietary lifestyle and a dead-foods lifestyle. We discussed the need for raw, ripe, fresh, organic produce. We highlighted the importance of transit time of your food to your mouth. The choice is and has always been yours. Every day you add more living foods back into your diet, you are adding more life, health, and vitality into your tomorrow.

* * * * *

6 CONVENIENCE VS. RIGHT

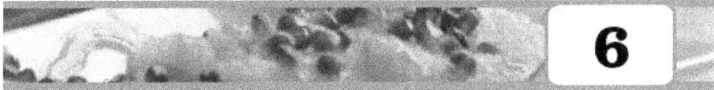

The choices we make daily impact our current and future health. Sadly, too many people today are basing their choices on convenience rather than what is right for long-term, sustainable, good health. In this chapter, we will take a look at the issue more and try to understand the current mindset and possible alternatives.

Have you ever had someone ask you a question that made you smile inside but on the outside you were really straight-faced as you tried to find a suitable answer? The most frequent sources of questions like that are from children ages 4 to 7. They ask the funniest questions but they are very sincere in their asking. So while you're smiling, you have to be very much sincere in your response to them.

I have had some times in my life when I have been asked such questions by adults. Sometimes I get the question, "is there a quick way to get rid of this weight?" I could say something like, "yes there is, if you are willing to spend the $4,000 to $10,000 to have a liposuction procedure done." I have worked in a plastic surgery clinic assisting in the OR and in post-OP so I know what those patients go through. And while I am happy to help out the surgeon in the OR, I would never recommend liposuction to anyone I cared about.

The procedure to me, is crude and brutal. After the surgeon completes plunging the stomach region, the other nurses and I are left to press on the stomach to push out all the fat, water, and blood from some lipo procedures. Sometimes, the surgeon has to cut away the excess skin in the stomach area, then rejoin the skin and create a new belly button for the patient.

It is a good idea for the patient to be asleep for such a procedure. And the patient always has bruising, pain and discomfort for days afterwards. For me, the cost in terms of emotional and physical well-being, and life-force is just too high to do that procedure, especially since I know of a better way to lose that weight.

Another question I sometimes get is, "is there an easy way to lose weight?" I might respond to that question by saying that the Lap-Band might be an option. I have not been involved in any way with such a procedure, so I can talk about it strictly from what I have read on the matter.

The Lap-Band is a prosthetic device made out of silastic, an inert material. This inert material has been used in medical devices for decades. Being inert means that it does not break down or deteriorate over time, which means that it can be left inside the body for life. The doctors do not worry about it breaking apart or degrading inside your body.

The name Lap-Band comes from the surgical technique used called the laparoscopic and also the name of the product used to tie the stomach i.e. the gastric band.

Using this procedure, your stomach gets turned into two parts, the upper stomach and the lower stomach. The Lap-Band Ring is the "belt" on the waist, if you can imagine it. When you eat a meal, the upper part fills with solid food and this causes you to feel full with a smaller portion of food. The stomach signals the brain that you are full so you don't overeat.

By creating an artificial feeling of being full, you can artificially starve yourself till you get smaller. You eat, thinking that you are eating normally. You feel full and therefore require smaller portions. You lose weight. Doesn't that sound easy enough?

Again, the Lap-Band procedure is not something that I would ever recommend to anyone I care about. It is another crude way to address the problem relating to one's diet. In fact, it does nothing to address the emotional linkage between food and comfort. But the procedure can be done in 30 to 45 minutes. How's that for convenience?

The final question I get asked a lot is, "isn't there some kind of pill that a person could take to lose the weight?". Maybe somewhere in the world there is such a pill, but I doubt it's safety and long-term weight-loss effectiveness.

People today seem to want the easy way out. Convenience is idolized and the mass media, marketing gurus, and retailers all try to pander to that growing trend.

Even the social media, Twitter, is born out of a need for a more convenient way to communicate text messages like phone text messages. That's why it has a 140-character limit. That was the size of a cell phone text message.

In today's society, anything and everything that makes life more convenient is desired, while things which do not add convenience to our lives are shunned, avoided and are generally not promoted for sale by anyone looking to make money.

Just think of this example. When you are driving in the city and you are getting all the green lights, you feel great. Everything is going smooth and is convenient. When you suddenly reach a traffic light, that momentum is broken.

You quickly get annoyed with the situation and even the city for not fixing this problem.

McDonald's is a fast-food restaurant that is known the world over. It is known not for its great tasting food or its healthy menu items. It is known for its standardization of the menu items and its convenience. It is conveniently located where people might need to eat and the food is the same worldwide.

But the question we need to ask ourselves is this: does having something convenient necessarily make it the right choice?

I would say that the more ways we add convenience into our lives, the more we create a dangerous lifestyle with long-term negative health implications. More convenience thus, equals more chances of sickness and disease.

Here is a list of some things that have added to our world of convenience:

Items of Convenience	
• Fridge	• Wireless Technology
• Microwave	• Convenience Stores
• Trains	• Convenience Housing
• Boats	• Bread maker
• Cars	• Toaster
• Cell phones	• Electric Scooters
• Walk-in Bath Tubs	• Cup holder
• Sit down toilets	• Tablets/Pills/Capsules

These are just a few of the things off the top of my head, but I am sure there are thousands of things in our lives that add the element of convenience.

Consider the refrigerator and how it has helped shape our eating habits. Fruits and vegetables are shipped in refrigerated containers, trucks, and boats. This slows their decomposition and slows the rate at which microbes can grow on them. The food can be shipped for days or weeks due to the fridge. It can be stored in the retail store for days. You can bring it in your home and store it for a few more days. Fruits and veggies which would have spoiled after a few days or a week can now last a month. Though the cellular decomposition is slow, the nutrient content and the phyto-nutrient content continues to degrade with time. The life energy of the food degrades with time. So your one-month-old, raw carrot is not as wholesome as a few-days-old, living carrot.

Microwave ovens are another device promoted as a way to add more convenience to people's lives. You can cook an entire meal in minutes from the comfort of your microwave oven. However, many do not realize the dangers of having foods destabilized on a cellular level. The resulting mutation of proteins, fats, and carbohydrates, all have an unwanted side effect on the body. Nuked food proteins and fats can become carcinogenic. The convenience of having a microwave prepare your food instead of cooking it yourself on your stove may be more harmful in the long term with respect to your health.

Cars are one more example I will use to show convenience. When you don't own a car, you walk everywhere. But once you own a car, you stop walking because driving is more convenient. And as a result, you begin to gain weight because you lose all those times when you got exercise from walking. Plus, the advent of cars has allowed people to live further away from the place where they work, so now they can spend two hours commuting to work. While I myself rely on a car to get around, I recognize that walking needs to be a conscious effort for the health-minded.

The advent of wireless technology is another convenience that people seem to be hooked on. Wireless allows people to have multiple devices connected at home, at work, at school, and allows everything to connect to the Internet. The cumulative effect of this continuous, daily bombardment of wireless frequencies is not fully understood and we are yet to see the results in the coming years.

While it is convenient to jump in the car to make a short trip to the local convenience store a block away, it is the right thing to just take a walk over there.

While it is convenient to have a wireless network at home with wireless video games, wireless speakers, wireless TV, wireless this or that, it is right to turn off those wireless emitters at night to allow your body to rest from the wi-fi waves.

Some conveniences are truly necessary to help with the quality of life and others are basically luxury items that we have. Thus, every person needs to assess for themselves whether each item of convenience is really worth it.

It is convenient to sit on your couch in your air-conditioned house, but it is right to go outside and get some exercise and breathe some fresh air.

It is convenient to eat an over-processed, chemically enhanced, standardized meal from a fast-food outlet but it is right to buy your fresh ingredients, prepare your own food, and enjoy it with love.

Summary of Chapter 6

In this chapter, we looked at the many ways society has become hooked on conveniences. We also discussed that what is convenient is not always right for our health in the long run.

Remember to make the right choices. Your health now and in the future depends on it.

* * * * *

7 A PROGRAM THAT WORKS

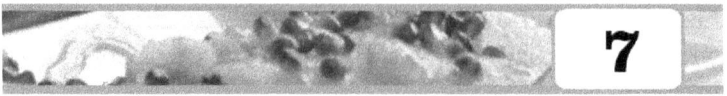

The Hippocrates Health Institute in West Palm Beach, Florida has been transforming lives for more than fifty years. Their program of education, along with alternative and holistic health, and living foods, is a proven success. My training at the institute was precisely the missing link between all my conventional medicine training and a holistic understanding of disease and well-being.

I recently read an article in the BBC news online about the weight-loss industry. The reporter asked the question about whether the industry is banking on failure, that is, on people to fail their diets and regain the weight. One startling statistic suggests that roughly 95% of dieters regain the weight.

The question could be asked, "If the weight-loss procedure worked perfectly, then how sustainable would the business be?" It's like the medical industry to some extent. If every doctor cured their patients, they would all be out of jobs eventually. So like medicine, it appears the real goal is to manage the disease or manage the weight, not get rid of it.

The article also reported that while there were no official statistics for spending on diet products, estimates vary from $40bn to $100bn in the USA alone. This is a phenomenal figure considering that the world is going through a recession.

The Hippocrates Health Institute program is different. The program is designed to help you get rid of what you've got. Losing weight is just a nice side effect once the body has regained its internal balance and homeostasis. One would think that such a program would eventually put the institute out of business, but this is not so. It is precisely because the rest of the world focus is on "managing", that to be focused on overcoming sickness and disease is sustainable. The institute's fifty-plus years in the industry has proven the case well.

My program developed at Eating4Eternity.org, is in part based on the Hippocrates Health Institute program. However, as I do not have the extensive assortment of equipment that they use, I limit the scope of patients. If someone is suffering from a chronic or terminal condition, then there is no substitute for going to the institute first.

The Eating4Eternity program serves two functions. Firstly, is to educate people about their options with regards to diet and lifestyle diseases. Many diseases can be traced back to a certain lifestyle. It is a simple cause and effect principle. If we alter the causative variable, then we can produce a different effect. Secondly, my program and my consultation aims at support in those from the Greater Toronto Area (GTA) and Ontario who have been to the institute already. I provide that extra avenue of support when you've left heaven on earth and are back in the real world.

Let's look at the basic components of the Eating4Eternity.org program.

Living Foods

Nutrition is a fundamental part of the program. The body is designed to function, given the correct balance of all the hormones, vitamins, minerals, fats, proteins, sugars, enzymes, and micro-nutrients. When one or more of the pieces are missing, then things in the body go out of whack. Then the body becomes weakened and susceptible to disease.

Thus, in any and all conditions of the body, a medical professional should never overlook the importance of nutrition. Unfortunately, all too often doctors do not ever take into consideration the role of diet in the onset or progression of a disease.

My program works from the basis that you are deficient from the beginning. By eating a healthier, living-foods diet, you will begin to give your body more sources of the nutrients from the variety of foods that you will be consuming.

As I mentioned in an earlier chapter, the white blood cells of the body are used to aid in digestion of cooked food, thus occupying them from their real job of fighting infection and disease. By ensuring that participants in our program are eating more raw - up to 75%, we are also reducing the stress on the immune system by the digestion process.

Exercise

Exercise is another fundamental pillar of this program. The body requires activity to keep it pulsing with vitality. Consider a person at sleep and a person who has just finished running an Olympic race. Would you see a difference in their behaviour? One would have little or no reaction while the other would be breathing, energetic, and filled with vitality.

We do promote exercise in the program but not the kind of "work yourself till you drop" exercise. We focus on exercise that helps the body to work out without straining the body. It can take some getting used to at first but the results are amazing.

Unfortunately, Canadians are not as active as we should be to foster good health.

Table 2: Canadian Exercise by Province

Province	% of Pop. Moderately Active
British Columbia	59
Yukon	58
Alberta	54
Ontario	53
Northwest Territories	52
Saskatchewan	50
Nova Scotia	49
Quebec	49
Manitoba	48
Nunavut	48
New Brunswick	46
Newfoundland & Labrador	46
Prince Edward Island	44
Overall Canadian Average	*49%*

(Source: Statistics Canada)

Overall, more than half of Canadians are lacking exercise. Why do you suppose this is? There are several reasons which converge to create an intense barrier to achieving the health benefits of regular exercise. Firstly, many people are just too busy with their work lives. When your job is 9 to 5 and it takes you 2 hours to get to work and 2 hours to get home after work, you've already spent 12 hours of your day. It's worse when you work a 12 hour shift like nurses in the hospital and then have to spend an hour or two extra going to and from work. So people are generally spending too much time on a job which requires little physical exercise.

The second reason that contributes to failure to exercise is that people spend their free time on activities that require no exercise, like watching TV or playing video games. Then, what little free time people have is wasted in activities which do nothing to stimulate the body and mind.

The third reason and probably the most important one is that very little value is placed on exercise. It is seen as a burden rather than a joy. People simply do not have the motivation and desire to exercise because in their mind, it is not a fun activity.

What's the solution to the convergence of these three factors? Firstly, one has to set limits on the amount of free time that will be spent watching TV or playing video games. This limit must be strictly enforced. Secondly, there are many ways to get exercise instead of just going to a gym. Walking is one of the best and cheapest types of exercise a person can do. We encourage walking along with some other targeted exercises in our program. As for the job, only you can decide if your job has become your life. If that is the case, then perhaps you need to consider a career change.

Oxygenation

Human beings need oxygen to carry out the biological functions necessary to give our bodies energy to live. Because too many people don't exercise, their breathing becomes very shallow. Over time, they are consistently under-nourishing their bodies with the improper supply of oxygen.

Most people take in just enough oxygen to prevent them from dying instead of taking in more oxygen to allow their body to thrive. So eventually sickness and disease creeps in because instead of thriving, the body is just surviving.

What is breathing? Breathing, called ventilation, consists of two separate phases. There is inspiration and expiration. During the phase called inspiration, the diaphragm and the external intercostal muscles contract. This causes the diaphragm to move downward, thereby increasing the volume of the thoracic (chest) cavity while the external intercostal muscles pull the ribs up and outward. The increased volume along with decreased air pressure inside the lungs causes air to flow into the lungs.

During the phase known as expiration, the diaphragm and external intercostal muscles both relax, causing a reduction in the size of the chest. This "shrinking" or returning-to-normal position creates a build-up of air pressure inside the lungs. This air pressure helps force carbon dioxide, water vapour, and other toxins out of the lungs and out of your body.

Rest & Relaxation

Resting and relaxation should be one of the easiest parts of any holistic health program, right? One would think that would be the case, but it has been my experience that many people are super stressed-out. The result is that they are unable to rest and relax in their daily lives. That is why this is a foundation component of my program. When you consider that rest and relaxation is one of the fundamental biological processes of life, then when a person neglects this, they are essentially neglecting a biological process they need for survival.

Could you imagine forgetting to breathe regularly or forgetting to use the toilet regularly? These are so important that our bodies urge us to take action at appropriate times or suffer the consequences. With rest and relaxation our bodies may not use hard-hitting signals, but the effects of long-term neglect of this are far reaching.

In my program, I focus on basic down-to-earth techniques for facilitating your rest and relaxation mechanism. Since I am not an expert in this area, I do also recommend some other techniques and/or practitioners who are better qualified in dealing with complex or chronic issues around one's inability to rest and relax.

Sunlight Nutrification

I made up the word nutrification, but used together with sunlight, I'll share the meaning. Sunlight nutrification recognizes the principle of the sunlight as a component of living. Indeed our bodies require sunlight food on a cellular level for proper function in a holistic manner.

By focusing on sunlight nutrification as a foundation of my program, we look at your intake of the sun's energy as nutrients and nutrition.

There are several ways to consider this, which I go into in my program, but one very simple approach, which is available freely to every human being on the planet, is getting more sunlight. In places that are naturally bright and sunny, like those located closer to the equator, sunlight nutrification is not an issue. However, for those of us living in places like Canada, which has a very cloudy and overcast winter season, this becomes a very real concern.

Water & Hydration

I could truly go on and on about water. I am very passionate about water. I believe that water is the most important bio-factor involved for our optimum health and wellness.

From the womb, where we as babies are being incubated, we are growing in an aqueous environment. At birth, our bodies are 90% water. And by the time people get to their old age and die, their bodies can get to as low as 50% water. The average adult is about 70% water.

I have given lectures again and again on the benefits of proper hydration and I closely follow the work of several health professionals in the field of water and hydration. For any person who is serious about their own health and who is serious about holistic health, water must be the foundation of everything. I am so passionate about water and the significance of it in health and wellness that I am considering doing a whole series on just water.

I encourage you to begin hydrating your body immediately. I also work with my clients systematically on how to go about hydrating their bodies for better function.

Spirituality

I touched on the power of the mind earlier in the book. But I want to help you take it even further by mentioning that having a deeply spiritual life in addition to a strong mind is supercharging to your health and wellness strategy.

A deeply spiritual person has a connection with their creator in a way that both grounds them in reality and lifts them to the supernatural. As a Christian, the belief in Jesus, Yeshua, or Messiah, has had a profound impact on the way many people have lived their lives for thousands of years. And the Jewish people found that their belief system has impacted their own lifestyle for hundreds of years prior to the birth of Jesus.

The old testament speaks of the prophets of old influencing the lives of the local people. Through those prophets, the God of Heaven and Earth was able to bring healing, abundance, recovery, joy, resurrection and more. And for many other people, their lives revolve around their personal belief system.

In my program, I am committed to help you take time to reconnect with your spirituality because of its importance as a tool in your health and wellness strategy. We consider where you are in your personal journey and highlight a path for you to consider in your journey.

A Good Holistic Health Professional

It is a good idea for anyone who is looking for a new direction in holistic health to work with a knowledgeable and proven health professional (conventional doctor or naturopathic doctor.) Think about this logically. If every patient a doctor has seen has died of disease X within one year and you have just been diagnosed with disease X. then if you make that doctor your doctor, what result can you expect within a year? Exactly. Now suppose your doctor is overweight and diabetic and you are going to her for type 2 diabetic treatment (reversible by the way), do you think you will be cured if your doctor hasn't cured herself?

You need to find a doctor or naturopath with a holistic health approach, who is truly progressive. I can probably recommend a few within the Toronto area, but for all the international readers, I recommend doing your research as I mentioned earlier. Check out their websites. Google any papers the professionals you're considering may have written. Look on Amazon to see if they have published anything. If you look and you can't find anything, then run to someone else. Please find a good doctor to work with. They will be your lifeline and support on your journey.

Summary of Chapter 7

In this chapter, we looked at the key factors involved in a holistic health and wellness program, and more specifically some of the things I promote in my own health and wellness coaching.

The fact is that health and wellness is everyone's personal responsibility, and by understanding the areas I have mentioned in this chapter and working through them, you will be able to get further on the path to health and wellness.

* * * * *

8 KEEPING IT ON BUDGET

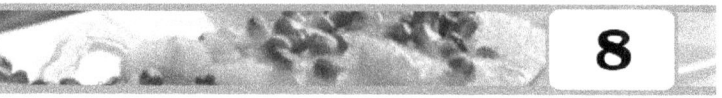

Money and personal finances are essential for anyone wishing to take up the journey on the path to health enlightenment. The world is such that good quality food is expensive while the poor quality food is cheap. But cheap food can cost you later in terms of a bigger medical bill, lost time, and other intangible costs, so you need to focus on your budget. We'll take a look at it here.

Having the money to be able to go to an expensive health institute is important when you need that type of help. Also, having the money to buy good, quality, organic food regularly is important. There are other things like the clothes you wear, the soaps and detergents you use in your home, the beds, carpets, and furnishings in your home, and others.

To get the non-toxic, good, quality items to replace the toxic, poor-quality items in your home will cost you money. At the beginning you may not have all that much money to invest in your health. Don't worry about it and allow it make you sick. I'll help you set priorities in this chapter.

Priority 1: Make a budget and stick to it no matter what

I have a dear friend who coincidentally wrote an article in the Winter 2012 issue of my magazine about how she and her husband were deeply in debt when they first got married. However, they were committed to good health and got control of their financial situation.

They managed to break free from their debt and now live much happier and healthier lives. Her advice was to make and live within a budget. This is really good advice. A budget can help you see where your money is going and also help you to redirect it in the proper way.

I also believe that too many people practice wasteful spending. They spend money on items that are not necessary for their long-term happiness and thus the money is wasted. With your budget, keep your bills and make note of your expenses. That way you'll be able to see where you are leaking money and fix the leak.

Priority #2: Make food a priority

The things going into your body are more important than the things you are putting on your body. I tell people that I don't buy new clothes for my body but would rather buy quality food for my body. I notice that some people love the latest fashion or the trendy-looking clothes while they are putting junk into their bodies.

I would recommend that people buy foods that are raw, ripe, fresh, and organic, and grown locally. These foods are more nutritious, and contain more of the vital life-force of the food that you want to consume when you eat it. Sometimes an exotic food like a durian or mango is nice to eat, but it is not the freshest because it has to be shipped here to Canada.

In making food your priority, there are a couple of ways to save money while going about this. One way is to create a small home garden and plant the vegetables, fruits, and greens that you will be using. I use square-foot gardening to try to get maximum yield for the land space that I have. The seeds are cheap (pennies to buy) and a well-cared-for crop will yield pounds of food, potentially saving you hundreds of dollars in your food bill.

Also, the farmer's markets are a great place to find quality, organic foods that are cheaper than in some of the pricier health food stores. I love the organic farmer's markets in Toronto and frequent them in the summer. You can find great prices from those farmers and the produce is fresh.

The third way is to join a Community Food Share group where local farms deliver a box of fresh organic produce for a fixed period over the summer and fall. You can save some money using these services and your time also, if they deliver.

I've given you three ways to start saving money on your food bill to ensure you get good-quality food into your body immediately and keep doing it going forward.

Priority #3: Make your home your priority

Many people live inside of their climate-controlled houses and don't allow fresh air into the house. You need to have a home that is properly ventilated during the day and night.

This can be done pretty cheaply by simply opening a window. It might be a challenge in the winter season, but you can leave it a tiny crack so that air is moving into and out of the house. If it gets too cold, then close it for a period, then open it again some hours later.

Priority #4: Make exercise a priority

Exercise has to become a priority and you can do it without breaking the budget on a gym membership.

Now, instead of taking your car on those short 5-minute drives to the corner store or the library, you should consider walking. This way, you will get back into the habit of walking regularly for your health.

Do you have a friend or family member with a condo that has a gym? Ask them if you can come by and use their condo gym once a week to do some toning and muscle-building. If they say yes, then you will have access to equipment on the cheap.

Also, you can do what the military does. They use anything in the environment as weight for muscle-building. They'll use logs, heavy rucksacks, and even other soldiers. You can get a bucket, and fill it with water or put in enough water so that you have to work at lifting it. Then do a few reps with it. It may seem old-fashioned but it can save you some cash.

Cancel your gym membership unless you have a personal trainer helping you to stay motivated, and use the free methods I've mentioned in this chapter.

Priority #5: Be financially responsible

If you know that you are abusing your credit cards, then cut them up and don't use them. Pay your credit card bills on time so that you avoid paying the interest fees. Don't buy things that you really cannot afford. Don't try to keep up with the Joneses - that means do not try to buy things just because your neighbour has them.

If you strive to live within the parameters of these five priorities in this chapter, you will be able to be in a better financial position to put yourself and your health in proper priority.

Summary of Chapter 8

In this chapter, we looked at some of the things you can do to get into a healthier lifestyle on a budget. I gave you five priorities which can help shape your financial focus and thus enhance your personal health and wellness goals.

* * * * *

9 SAMPLE MEAL PLAN

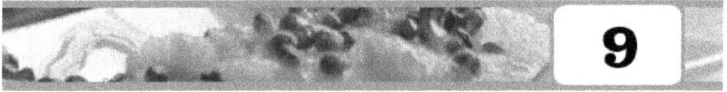

This chapter will attempt to give you a brief overview of a healthy and healthful eating/meal plan. You should take into account that no single meal plan will work for everyone. This is because everyone has had different influences in their lives which have impacted their biological makeup. Added to this, with the different age and affluence level of each person, you will find that it becomes difficult to create a one-size-fits-all meal plan. However, even with all the differences between communities, families and individuals, there are a few baseline commonalities that we all have. Thus, this meal plan can be considered as the bare-bones or baseline. This meal plan is also the first step. A review of your meal plan should be done within 2 to3 months and modified again as your body changes. A qualified naturopath or holistic nutritionist can help you. You will need to add more or supplement, depending on your own personal circumstances.

Key elements of this plan:
- Detoxification: We begin with the assumption that everyone has toxins in their body, either from birth or accumulated during the course of their daily living. Based on this underlying assumption, the diet will contain an element of detoxification.
- Dehydration: We begin with the assumption that everyone is operating with a sub-optimal water intake protocol. That is, we believe that everyone is not drinking enough water at the time necessary for optimal health.

- Malnourishment: Here, we make the assumption that everyone is facing some kind of malnourishment, ever if their body is overweight, because an optimally functioning body does not need to accumulate excess fat beyond that necessary for survival.

Phase 1: Substitution Protocol

In this phase, you will begin to substitute everything unhealthy in your diet with healthier options.

Item	Substitute
Coffee, Tea, Pop/Soda	Water
Processed Juices From Concentrate, Juice Mixes	Pure Organic and Fresh Squeezed Juices
White/Whole Wheat flour, white/brown rice, white/whole wheat breads	Barley, Millet, Quinoa, Sprouted-Grain Breads
Dairy products	Organic, plant-based substitute
Processed Snacks	Whole raw nuts and seeds
Tinned Beans and Legumes	Organic Beans and Legumes

Notice in the substitution phase, you are replacing the highly processed and nutrient-deficient food items with healthier, whole-food, organic items. This should be done for as much of your diet as possible. The goal of this phase is to substitute the unhealthy items with more wholesome and healthier options.

Phase 2: Addition Protocol

This phase will see the introduction of items that you probably have not eaten much of before. You will add the items listed below into your diet. Note if you have a specific illness that presents a contraindication with the suggested items, then please consult a qualified expert on the topic for further advice. For example, green juices help to thin the blood and oxygenate the cells, so anyone on prescription blood thinners needs to be extremely careful that their blood does not get too thin which raises risks of internal bleeding or too much bleeding for an external cut. I would suggest talking to your doctor to let her know that you are starting more greens and asking if they would consider reducing your dosage once they check you out.

Items To Add Into Your Diet:
- Green Vegetables: You should eat more leafy green vegetables in your diet.
- Green Juices: Drink more vegetable juices containing lots of leafy green vegetables.
- Raw Garlic: Garlic is an excellent anti-microbial food. You could add one garlic clove or half of a clove to your daily diet for 10-12 days. Mix it with your green juice or eat it with a salad.
- Fresh Wheatgrass Juice: Most people don't have wheatgrass on hand, so that will most likely be available from a local juice bar. Do not exceed more than one ounce per day on an empty stomach for this juice. It takes getting used to and a good quality juice should taste slightly sweet. For those with allergies to wheat, the juice from the grass should be no problem. Test a couple of drops on your skin and/or consult an allergist to be sure.

Will you get enough calcium? At Harvard University, they have undertaken an extensive look at the linkage between milk, calcium, and the risk of more fractures (due to weaker bones). One study indicated that, "male health professionals and female nurses, individuals who drank one glass of milk (or less) per week were at no greater risk of breaking a hip or forearm than were those who drank two or more glasses per week." Another study found, "no association between calcium intake and fracture risk." The source is: http://www.hsph.harvard.edu/nutritionsource/what-should-you-eat/calcium-full-story/

With an increased intake of the greens and green vegetable juices, you will have a good intake of bio-available calcium. The study also recommends that vitamin D is necessary for the proper absorption of calcium, so you should have a whole-food source of vitamin D from your local health food store or get it from the sun for free.

Daily Meal Plan Sample

[0:00] Wake Up	Drink 2 to 3 cups of water.
[0:30] Juice	1 to 2 cups fresh veggie juice
[1:20] Water	1 to 2 cups water
[2:00] Breakfast*	Fruit
[3:30] Water	1 to 2 cups water
[5:00] Lunch*	Large salad plus small meal
[7:00] Water	1 to 2 cups water
[8:00] Juice	1 to 2 cups fresh veggie juice
[9:00] Water	1 to 2 cups water
[10:00] Dinner*	Small salad plus small meal
[11:30] Water	½ cup to 1 cup water
[12:00] Rest*	Go To Bed

* These times can be adjusted up to 1 hour later to help fit your schedule. The timings for all other activities following would then be later according to the adjustment.

For example, if lunch is pushed to [6:00 hr] then Water becomes [8:00 hr] and so on for the remainder of the schedule. Note that dinner should not be eaten any later than 30 minutes after sunset.

To use the daily plan, try this example. If you wake up at 6:00 am, then [0:00] equals 6 am. The next time on the chart [0:30] would be equal to 6:30 am and so on, until [12:00] would be equal to 6:00pm.

You will note that the daily plan includes a lot of water drinking. The purpose of this is to get back into hydrating your body at an optimum level. You should be drinking a minimum of ½ your body weight in ounces of water. Thus a 200 lb person should drink a minimum of 100 oz of water per day. The schedule will help you build water drinking into your routine.

Important! Persons with any bladder or kidney conditions need to consult their doctor to find safe levels of water intake. Persons unable to urinate frequently should also check with their doctor for a proper protocol. With too much water intake when faced with the types of conditions mentioned, there is a risk of water retention and drowning the heart. So it is important to be sure you are urinating properly. The risk of too little water intake (dehydration) is the onset of many lifestyle diseases, from migraines to joint pains. Thus, you must find the correct balance for your body and personal health circumstance.

Weekly Meal Plan Sample

Weekly Meal Plan Sample

Sunday	Cook (up to 50% raw meal | raw soup)
Monday	Raw Day (80-100% raw meal)
Tuesday	Cook (up to 50% raw meal)
Wednesday	Raw
Thursday	Cook
Friday	Raw
Saturday	Vegetable Juice or Water Fast

Recipes

When you are starting this path which includes dietary change, it is always helpful to have a few easy recipes to help you get started. It is my intent to give you a sample set of recipes to help with transitioning as well as eating raw. You will find some recipes that contain partially cooked and raw ingredients. You will also find a couple of fully cooked recipes which are vegan. This is intentional. These recipes will be identified as such and are useful for your transition days. Note: A glossary of terms for different ingredients can be found at the end of this chapter.

You can mix and match the recipes that appeal to you on your transition days or raw days. I'd say, try your best not to eat a 100% cooked meal on a raw day. I'd also recommend you try your best to eat an 80-100% raw meal on the raw days.

Five (5) Breakfast Meal Options

1. Sacha Inchi Milkshakes
2. Berries Milkshakes
3. Greens Smoothies
4. Superpower Cereals
5. Coconut Banana Pancakes

#1: *Sacha Inchi Milkshake*

This is an excellent drink to use as a meal replacer in the morning.

Preparation Level: Beginner
Category: Drink
Equipment: Blender
Rawness: 95%
Serves: 1

Ingredients

½ cup Sacha Inchi seeds
¼ cup raw hemp seeds
1 Tbsp coconut oil
1 Tbsp vanilla extract
3 pitted dates (soaked)
1 ripe banana
1 1/2 cup alkaline water (pH 8.5)

Put hemp seeds, Sacha Inchi seeds, dates in a bowl of water and soak for 2 hrs. In a blender, combine all the ingredients and blend until smooth and creamy. Serve immediately.

#2: *Berries Milkshake*

This is an excellent drink to use as a meal replacer in the morning.

Preparation Level: Beginner
Category: Drink
Equipment: Blender
Rawness: 95%
Serves: 1

Ingredients

2 cups almond milk
½ cups strawberries
½ cup raspberries

½ cup wild blueberries
1 ripe banana
1 Tbsp flax oil
1 Tbsp coconut oil

In a blender, combine all the ingredients and blend until smooth and creamy. Serve immediately.

#3: Green Smoothie
This is a wonderful smoothie that is packed with green goodness.
Preparation Level: Beginner
Category: Drink
Equipment: Blender
Rawness: 100%

Ingredients
4 fresh large kale leaves
1 cup cilantro leaves, chopped
½ bunch green lettuce
2 pitted dates (soaked)
1 ½ cup alkaline water (pH 8.5)

In a blender, combine all the ingredients and blend until smooth. Serve immediately.

#4: Superpower Cereal
This is a wonderful cereal that is packed with yummy flavor.
Preparation Level: Beginner
Category: Breakfast Meal
Equipment: Knife
Rawness: 90%
Serves: 1

Ingredients
2 Tbsp chia seeds
4 Tbsp hemp seeds

2 Tbsp flax meal
¼ cup almond milk
½ scoop Sun Warrior powder
½ scoop Vega powder
1 banana
½ cup strawberries
½ cup wild blueberries

In a small bowl, soak chia seeds in almond milk for 15 minutes. The chia will swell and become soft in texture. Then add hemp seeds, flax meal, Sun Warrior powder, Vega powder, and almond milk together. Stir them well. Cut the banana into small chunks and sprinkle on the cereal with strawberries and blueberries. This cereal will keep you going for hours without feeling hungry again.

#5: Coconut Banana Pancake
This is a tasty cooked alternative to the traditional milk and dairy pancake.
Preparation Level: Beginner
Category: Breakfast Meal
Equipment: Bowl, Frying Pan/Skillet
Rawness: 0% (Cooked Recipe)
Serves: 2

Ingredients
1 ¼ cup whole wheat pastry flour
2 tsp baking powder
2 Tbsp coconut palm nectar
pinch sea salt
¼ cup grated coconut
1 cup almond milk (can use up to half coconut milk)
1 ripe banana, mashed
¼ cup coconut oil

In a bowl, combine the flour, baking powder, sea salt, grated coconut and sweetener. Stir well. Add coconut oil, mashed banana, and almond milk together. Fold in the batter well. In a skillet, lightly oil the pan and ladle on some pancake mixture. Bake on one side 5 minutes until bubbles appear on the top of the pancake; flip to the other side for 5 minutes to bake until browned. Serve with almond butter or drizzle some maple syrup if desired.

Eight (8) Lunch/ Dinner Meal Options

1. Classic Yellow Split Pea Soup
2. Warming Beta-carotene Soup
3. Sweet Tomatoes and Basil Soup (raw)
4. Calcium-Rich Veggies
5. Marinated Kale Salad (raw)
6. Rainbow Beans Veggie Salad
7. Sprouted Salad (raw)
8. Meatless Beans Stew

#1: Classic Yellow Split Pea Soup
This is a wonderful and delicious soup that is great at lunch or dinner.
Preparation Level: Beginner
Category: Main Meal
Equipment: Knife, Soup Pot, Grater
Rawness: 0% (Cooked Meal)

Ingredients
1 cup yellow split peas
5 cups water
4 garlic cloves, finely chopped or grated
¼ cup onion, chopped fine
1 tsp turmeric powder
1 tsp cumin powder
½ tsp fresh ginger, finely chopped or grated
sea salt to taste
¼ cup coconut oil

Soak the yellow split peas overnight and rinse off several times in the morning.

In a skillet, add coconut oil, grated garlic, grated ginger, turmeric, cumin powder, cut onion and sea salt to sauté for 10 minutes until it turns golden brown. Then transfer the yellow split peas and sauté for another 15 minutes while stirring a few times; then add water to cover the peas. Allow to simmer for 1 ½ hours or until the split peas are soft and breaking apart. Serve with brown rice or a slice of multigrain or sprouted bread with salad on the side.

#2: *Warming Beta-carotene Soup*

This is a wonderful and delicious soup that is great at lunch or dinner.

Preparation Level: Beginner
Category: Main Meal
Equipment: Knife, Soup Pot, Grater
Rawness: 0% (Cooked Meal)

Ingredients

1 cup carrot, peeled and cubed
1 cup butternut squash, peeled and cubed
1 cup sweet potatoes, peeled and cubed
1 cup pumpkin, peeled and cubed
6 Tbsp coconut oil or olive oil
½ cup celery, cubed
1 medium onion, diced
1 inch fresh ginger
1 bay leaf
1 tsp fresh thyme
1 tsp fresh sage
2 cups vegetable stock
2 garlic cloves
sea salt and black pepper to season
½ to 1 cup non-dairy milk (almond, rice or soya milk)

Optional:

1 cup chopped walnut pieces
2 Tbsp maple syrup
1 tsp fresh rosemary, chopped
pinch cayenne pepper and salt

Bake the carrot, butternut squash, sweet potatoes and pumpkin in preheated oven at 375° F for 45 minutes or until tender.

In a skillet pan, add coconut oil, onion, garlic, sage, thyme, bay leaf, celery, ginger, salt and pepper to sauté for 10 minutes. Add vegetable stock and bring to a boil; reduce heat to simmer for 30 minutes. Discard bay leaf. When baked carrot, sweet potatoes, butternut squash, and pumpkin are cool enough, transfer into the blender with the puree soup mixture and almond milk. Blend until smooth and creamy. Serve with multigrain bread or a salad on the side.

In a skillet over low heat, add walnut, maple syrup, salt, cayenne pepper and rosemary. Cook for about 2 minutes, stirring frequently until the syrup is caramelized and nuts are toasted. Be careful not to burn the nuts. Let cool. Sprinkle on top of the soup. Walnuts are a very good source of protein, fibre, folic acid, vitamin B6, magnesium, phosphorus and an excellent source of omega 3 fatty acids, which have anti-inflammatory properties.

This is a warming soup full of alpha and beta carotene, rich in the vibrant color of fall. When fall season approaches, we find different types of squashes, pumpkins, and yams greet us with the warmth of sunshine. This soup helps us fight free radicals, protects the heart, guards against cancer and is full of vitamin C, fibre and lutein.

#3: Sweet Tomatoes and Basil Soup

This is a wonderful and delicious soup that is great at lunch or dinner.

Preparation Level: Beginner
Category: Main Meal
Equipment: Knife, Soup Pot, Grater

Rawness: 100%

Ingredients
1 lb ripe tomatoes
1 ripe red bell pepper
1 ripe yellow bell pepper
1 clove of garlic
2 tsp lemon juice
2 cups alkaline water (pH 8.5)
1 cup raw sundried tomatoes
1/4 tsp chipotle powder
1/4 cup fresh basil, finely chopped

Cut the red and yellow bell peppers into square pieces. Place half of each into the blender. Add the cut tomatoes into the blender with the water. Add the sundried tomatoes, garlic, lemon juice and half the basil. Puree everything in the blender until a creamy liquid.

Pour the liquid into a bowl and add the rest of the dry ingredients. Mix and serve immediately.

#4: Calcium-Rich Veggies
This is a wonderful and delicious salad that is great at lunch or dinner.
Preparation Level: Beginner
Category: Main Meal
Equipment: Knife
Rawness: 100%

Ingredients
1 cup kale leaves, chopped fine
1 cup green lettuce, chopped fine
1 cup cucumber, sliced
1 cup sweet cherry tomatoes, cut into half
½ cup parsley, chopped fine
½ cup cilantro, chopped fine
¼ cup red onion, thinly sliced

1 garlic clove, thinly sliced

Prepare all the ingredients and set aside into a bowl. Add salad dressing to toss and coat well.

This veggie salad is not only full of greens colors, but it is also full of calcium. Greens are among our best bone-builders and have alkalizing health benefits. Load your plate with green veggies for better bone health.

#5: Marinated Kale Salad

This is a wonderful and delicious salad that is great at lunch or dinner.

Preparation Level: Beginner
Category: Main Meal
Equipment: Knife, Blender
Rawness: 100%

Red Pepper un-Cheeze Dressing Ingredients

1 sweet red pepper
1 Tbsp lemon juice
2 Tbsp nutritional yeast
1 Tbsp nama shoyu
1 tsp raw apple cider vinegar
½ tsp sea salt
½ tsp Cajun seasonings
½ cup water
1 cup raw cashews or sunflower seeds
pinch of cayenne pepper
2 dates (soaked) or 1 Tbsp sweetener

Blend everything in the blender until it's smooth and creamy. Transfer into a mason jar and keep in the fridge for 1 week. Can be use as salad dressing or marinade.

Kale Salad Ingredients

½ bunch of curly kale leaves, chopped into pieces
1 cup sweet cherry tomatoes, cut into half
2 avocados, chopped and cubed

¼ cup red onion, thinly sliced
¼ cup hemp seeds

Remove stems from kale leaves and chop into small pieces. Combine the dressing sauce and massage a few times until it looks like cooked kale. Add tomatoes, avocados, onion and hemp seeds together and mix them well. This salad is very filling and loaded with chlorophyll green.

#6: Rainbow Beans Veggie Salad
This is a wonderful and delicious bean salad that is great at lunch or dinner.
Preparation Level: Beginner
Category: Main Meal
Equipment: Knife, Soup Pot, Bowl
Rawness: 50% (Raw & Cooked Meal)

Ingredients
¾ cup kidney beans
¾ cup pinto beans
¾ cup northern white beans
¾ cup black beans
1 cup cooked rainbow shell pasta
4 garlic cloves
1 medium onion
4 Tbsp coconut oil
1 Tbsp Italian seasonings
1 cup sweet red pepper, cubed
1 cup sweet yellow and orange pepper, cubed
½ cup red onion, cubed
½ cup cilantro, chopped fine
½ cup parsley, chopped fine
½ cup fresh basil, chopped fine
2 Tbsp flax oil
3 Tbsp coconut oil or olive oil
sea salt and pepper to season

1 Tbsp lemon juice

Soak the dried beans in a large bowl overnight. Rinse and drain off excess water. In a large pot, put 5 cups of water and add the beans to boil until soft. Drain off the water and set the beans aside to cool.

In a skillet, add onion, garlic, Italian seasonings, sea salt, and coconut oil to sauté for 10 minutes. In a small pot, add 2 cups of water and pasta together to bring to a boil until the pasta is cooked. Drain finished pasta and allow to cool.

Prepare the raw ingredients, sweet peppers, onion, cilantro, parsley, basil, lemon juice, sea salt, pepper, flax oil and olive oil in a large bowl, toss well. Transfer the cooked pasta, and cooked beans with the sautéed seasoning together and mix them well.

#7: Sprouted Salad

This is a wonderful and delicious sprouted salad that is great at lunch or dinner.

Preparation Level: Beginner
Category: Main Meal
Equipment: Knife, Bowl
Rawness: 100%

Ingredients
4 Tbsp Crunch Mixed Beans (sprouting bean mix)
4 Tbsp mung beans
1 cup microgreens
1 cup mixed field greens
4 Tbsp olive oil
2 Tbsp flax oil
2 Tbsp toasted sesame oil
1 tsp lemon juice
1 cup sweet cherry tomatoes
1 avocado, cubed
¼ cup red onion, thinly sliced
1 Tbsp garlic powder
1 Tbsp onion powder

½ Tbsp cumin powder
pinch sea salt and cayenne pepper
1 Tbsp nama shoyu
1 Tbsp nutritional yeast (optional)
2 Tbsp hemp seeds

Soak the mung beans and crunch beans mixed in 2 separate mason jars overnight. Rinse off the water several times and leave it on the counter to sprout for 2 days or until you see tiny shoots coming out of the beans. Rinse the beans twice a day, once in the morning and once in the evening.

You can purchase prepared field greens salad from the supermarket and microgreens from places that sell sprouts, like organic groceries and health food stores.

In a small bowl, add garlic powder, onion powder, cumin, sea salt, nama shoyu, cayenne pepper, olive oil, flax oil, sesame oil, lemon juice together and give it a couple of whisks to mix them well.

On serving plate, add the field greens, microgreens, the sprouted beans, sweet tomatoes, avocados and red onion and drizzle the dressing; toss and coat well. You can sprinkle nutritional yeast to add a cheesy taste and hemp seeds for Omega-3 fatty acids.

#8: Meatless Bean Stew

This is a wonderful and delicious meatless stew that is great at lunch or dinner.

Preparation Level: Beginner
Category: Main Meal
Equipment: Knife, Bowl, Pot
Rawness: 0% (Cooked Meal)

Ingredients

4 Tbsp Crunch Mixed Beans (sprouting beans)
1 cup oyster mushrooms, cubed
2 cups northern white beans

1 cup potatoes, cubed
1 cup sweet potatoes, cubed
1 cup carrots, cubed
4 garlic cloves
½ cup onion, chopped fine
4 Tbsp coconut oil
1 Tbsp cumin powder
pinch sea salt
pinch cayenne pepper
1 Tbsp fresh thyme
1 Tbsp fresh rosemary

Soak the dried beans overnight. Rinse and drain off excess water. In a small pot, add 3 cups of water with the beans to bring to a boil until cooked. Drain off the water and set the beans aside.

In a skillet, add coconut oil, garlic, onion, thyme, rosemary, sea salt, pepper, cumin, and cayenne pepper to sauté for 10 minutes; then add potatoes, carrots, and sweet potatoes to sauté for 15 minutes. Add ½ cup water to cook until tender for 20 minutes.

Add the oyster mushrooms last to cook for 10 minutes. Now combine the cooked white beans, the potato stew and oyster mushroom together. Mix them up. Can be served with brown rice, quinoa grains, millet grains, or just a toasted bread with a garden salad on the side.

Note: The oyster mushrooms just taste like chewy meat instead of having a traditional beef stew. They have a rich, meaty texture and a savoury, intense flavour.

Four (4) Fantastic Drink Options

1. Citrus and Vitamin C Booster Shot
2. Nut Punch
3. Colon Energizer
4. Better-Than-Coffee Drink

These drinks are so yummy and filling that they can be used to provide your body with nutrients when you're in a rush. You can also pack them with you in a cold container for drinking later.

Drink #1: Citrus & Vitamin C Booster Shot

This is an excellent fresh juice that your body will appreciate and love you for. It can help give your body fresh bio-available vitamin C.

Preparation Level: Beginner
Category: Drink
Equipment: Blender, Citrus Juicer
Rawness: 100%

Ingredients

2 organic ripe oranges
1 organic ripe grapefruit
1/2 medium-sized lemon
1 inch of fresh ginger root
pinch of cinnamon powder
1 Tbsp organic sweetener (date paste or agave)
1 cup alkaline water (pH 8.5)

Juice the oranges, grapefruit, and lemon using your citrus juicer. Set aside juice. Add ginger, water, and cinnamon to the blender and blend until smooth. Mix both liquids together and serve. Add the sweetener if the juice is too sour. Drink the juice immediately.

Drink #2: Seedy Nut Punch

A really tasty nut punch can be a good source of protein and can be very filling. This nut punch is great as a snack, but don't drink too much as you might gain weight.

Preparation Level: Beginner
Category: Drink
Equipment: Blender

Rawness: 95%

Ingredients
2 cups hemp milk
1/4 cup organic almonds
1/4 cup pumpkin seeds
1/4 cup sesame seeds
1/4 cup dates (soaked)
Optional flavoring*

Soak all the seeds and the almonds for 3 to 4 hours for better digestion. Drain and rinse the almonds and seeds. Place all the ingredients in the blender and blend until smooth. If the liquid is too thick, then add a little water to loosen it a bit. For the optional flavoring, you can add a 1/4 tsp of cinnamon, or carob powder.

Drink #3: Colon Energizer
Your colon needs to be hydrated and well nourished in order to maintain its health. You need to have regular bowel movements. This drink is a nice addition to your colon health.
Preparation Level: Beginner
Category: Drink
Equipment: Blender
Rawness: 100%

Ingredients
1 cup papaya
2 peeled oranges
1 to 2 cups alkaline water (pH 8.5)

Blend everything in the blender until it is liquefied. If the drink is too thick, you can add extra water so that it is easier to drink. Drink all of it.

Drink #4: Better-Than-Coffee Drink

Coffee is one of the most popular stimulants on the planet. People develop a dependency on it because their bodies are already over-worked, over-tired and poorly nourished. This "Better-Than-Coffee Drink" is a great substitute that will get you going.

Preparation Level: Beginner
Category: Drink
Equipment: Blender
Rawness: 70%

Ingredients
1 cup peppermint tea (room temperature)
1/2 cup soaked hazelnuts
1 Tbsp organic sweetener
1 cup alkaline water (pH 8.5)

Blend the nuts and water together until creamy. Add the tea and the sweetener and blend until mixed.

Two (2) Exquisite Dressings

1. Sweet Mustard Salad Dressing
2. Citrus Hemp Salad Dressing

You will be using a lot of salads on this program, but salads do not need to be boring at all. I've included two of my favorite dressings to help make your salad more enjoyable.

Dressing #1: Sweet Mustard Salad Dressing

This is an excellent homemade dressing. My Sweet Mustard raw dressing is a hit at the raw food potlucks.

Preparation Level: Beginner
Category: Dressing
Equipment: Blender

Rawness: 95%

Sweet Mustard Dressing Ingredients
1 cup raw organic hemp hearts
2 Tbsp organic garlic powder or 1 clove garlic
4 Tbsp raw organic agave nectar
2 Tbsp raw nama shoyu
1 Tbsp organic Italian seasonings
1/4 cup raw organic red onion
1 Tbsp organic mustard powder
1/4 cup alkaline water (pH 8.5)

Blend everything in the blender until it is creamy and smooth. Pour it on any salad. You can keep the balance in fridge for up to 3 days.

Dressing #2: Citrus Hemp Dressing

Preparation Level: Beginner
Category: Dressing
Equipment: Blender
Rawness: 90%

Citrus Hemp Dressing
1 cup raw organic hemp hearts
1/4 cup fresh-squeezed raw organic orange juice
1/4 cup Meyer lemon juice
1/4 cup cold-pressed olive oil
1 Tbsp Italian seasoning
1 Tbsp onion powder
1 Tbsp garlic powder or 1 clove garlic
1 Tbsp raw agave nectar
1 Tbsp raw nama shoyu
10 fresh organic basil leaves
1/2 Tsp sea salt
1/4 cup alkaline water (pH 8.5)

Blend everything until smooth and creamy in the blender. This can be used as a salad dressing or can also be used as a marinade for any veggie.

Glossary of Terms

Alkaline Water: This is water with a pH value greater than 7. I mention pH 8.5 in some of the recipes. This is the pH of Spring water and water from some water ionizer devices.

Almond Milk: This is the milk you make not the store bought version which has too much sugar added (even the unsweetened version). Same for hemp milk.

Crunch Mixed Beans: This is a packet of various seeds for sprouting.

Nama Shoyu: This is a raw soy sauce. Make sure you can find organic as soy is highly sprayed or genetically modified.

Summary of Chapter 9

In this chapter, we looked at the importance of eating correctly. I showed you a sample meal plan that will help you put back nutrients as well as water into your body. I also provided you with some of my favourite recipes as samples to help get you started on the way.

*****

10 A GLIMPSE OF THE FUTURE

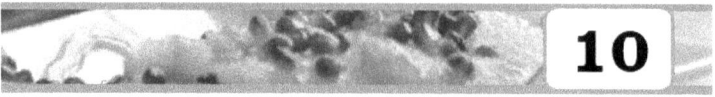

Throughout this book, I have taken you on a journey of health and wellness. I have showed you an overview of our medical industry on a macro level, and have drilled down into the personal level, or micro level.

Now you stand at a crossroads in your own life. Will you take everything that you have learned within these pages and do something to improve your life and make it better OR will you simply ignore everything you have learned in this book? Will you attempt to dismiss it with some of the flimsy excuses that have been used time and time again by those not really wanting to improve their health?

This chapter for you, can be compared to that scene in the hugely popular movie, The Matrix, starring Keanu Reeves. In the early part of the movie, the character Morpheus, explains to Keanu's character, Neo, that the world they are living in is a lie. Morpheus shows Neo that the human being is now being kept in farms in a dormant state where only their minds are active. But their reason for existing is to provide bio-electric power for the machines that keep the human species captive.

After learning these truths, Morpheus tells Neo, that he has a choice which consists of two options. He presents Neo with two pills, one red and the other blue.

One pill will cause Neo to forget about everything he has learned and he can return to life in what he hopes to be a normal existence. The other pill takes Neo deeper into the path of enlightenment that he has begun. But whichever choice he makes, there is no turning back.

Neo, the hero of the story, chooses to take the pill which goes forward into the path of enlightenment. You are at the same crossroad here. Unfortunately I have no pill to give you, but nevertheless, the choice is set before you this day.

Today is the day that you must choose. Will you choose life, and then act to live it more abundantly or will you choose death and carry out your lifestyle to fulfill your choice?

I would personally like you to choose life because every moment of your life is called the present. It is a present and a gift to you. Why not live your life as you were meant to : in good health and abundance?

Just in case you are still in doubt about what the future can hold, let me paint a best-case scenario of what life with heaven on earth could be like.

First, the person who takes full responsibility for their health and wellness makes it a point to learn about the functions of the human body and indeed their own body. They are always curious about why things happen the way they do in the body. They read books, websites, and search out knowledge which answers their questions.

Second, the person who chooses a life on the path to health and wellness enlightenment, does not let every fad disease, or threat of disease frighten them. Swine flu has no sting. The threat of a horrible flu season has no fear factor. The health and wellness-conscious person is confident, and this confidence is borne from a position of full knowledge, not of ignorance.

Third, a person with control of their health and wellness destiny, can address many of the minor medical ailments with confidence and boldness. They know that dis-ease A has root causes of B and/or C. And they take steps to remove the causative factors and allow the time for the wonderfully designed human body to act towards the reversal of the condition.

Fourth, a person with health consciousness, is at peace with themselves and at harmony with nature. They do not seek to kill or destroy animals and are not interested in behaviours which promote chaos and disharmony. They respect the life of the individual and the life of the animals. Their lifestyle reflects this belief.

Fifth, a health-minded person is not a burden to the medical system, to their family, or to themselves by their deliberate actions of promoting ill health in themselves. I see people who come to the ER with common colds or migraines or other simple problems that could easily be remedied at home if they were knowledgeable. This of course, does not include people who are ill due to some unavoidable situation. A health-minded person chooses healthy foods, attitudes, and a lifestyle aligned with the principles of good health.

Sixth, a health-conscious person is an asset to everyone around them. These individuals are exactly like a person who knows CPR in a crowded room where someone is in need of assistance. When people who lack the knowledge need a remedy, these folks are there, capable and able to help.

In a world where people who fit these characteristics exist, you will see some amazing ripples. Consider a few of these examples:

- Hospital emergency rooms would not be filled with people who show up for the simplest things which then create long wait times for people with more serious needs.
- Employers would see the benefit of lower health insurance premiums for their staff.
- Companies would see more productive staff and reduced sickness and absences due to poor lifestyle choices.
- Insurance companies would not have to be worried about people who focus on health, and so could reduce the premiums and the risks.
- Communities would benefit from educated and health-conscious members who actively promote a higher standard of living.
- Companies that produce quality products that enhance life and promote long life, health, and vitality, would see enormous benefits.
- Companies that produce poor quality, disease causing stuff, would be forced to change that business purpose to align with their customers or face going out of business.

This kind of perfect utopia may be far away from us collectively in the present time, but as individuals, each of us can impact our own life and the lives of those in close proximity to us. And if you choose the path of health enlightenment, then this could be the fulfillment of it in your micro-world.

The alternative is to live a life of health mediocrity and just go along with the flow. You allow yourself to become disease-riddled and suffer reduced quality of life as you get older until one day you wish for death because living is just too much of a burden. This is totally opposite to what the human being was designed for. But you are the ultimate master of your destiny and you control the choice that you will make and the actions that will follow that decision.

In closing, I want you to know that my 20-plus years in the medical industry has shown me all types of scenarios and I've been blessed to laugh and cry with my patients. I've had the chance to be a comforter, an advocate, a listening ear, and a sounding board.

I want you, as much as I want every single patient, person, friend, family member, reader of my magazine or blog, or anyone else I come into contact with to have a better life.

I want you to have a life worth living. So I'll leave you with my love and my sincere best wishes for you. Peace and be well. – Jenny.

MORE RESOURCES

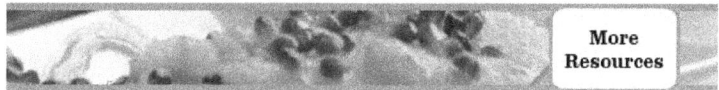

EternityWatch Magazine
(www.eternitywatchmagazine.com)

EternityWatch Magazine is the premier magazine for those seeking a truly holistic approach to health and wellness. The magazine is founded on the belief that good health is everyone's birthright and that by proper education, people can make the right choices to maintain their good health. We focus on quality-length articles on all aspects of holistic health, sustainable living, eco-conscious living, and organic, plant-based nutrition. We also cater to the rapidly growing vegan, and raw/living foods movement. ***Get A FREE copy of the magazine on the site.***

Eating4Eternity.org
(www.eating4eternity.org)

Eating4Eternity is founded by Jenny Berkeley and is focused on her personal coaching approach. On the site, you will find news articles on health and wellness, Jenny's blog posts with her personal insights into what is happening in the medical field, and some free information.

Hippocrates Health Institute
(www.hippocratesinst.org)

Hippocrates Health Institute is the premier institute for alternative health and wellness. With over 50 years of experience in educating people to take control of their health destiny, the institute has a solid foundation. Their website talks about their programs, plus you can find copies of their magazine.

* * * * *

ABOUT THE AUTHOR

Jenny Berkeley is a registered nurse and health educator. She has worked both locally in Canada and internationally. She is a tiny gal with a big heart that she wears on her sleeve. Jenny has over 20 years of experience in the medical profession caring for her patients, being their advocate, and supporting her colleagues.

In addition to her medical background, she is an author, speaker, lecturer, and blogger. Her Twitter following is now over 38,000. She is also the co-founder and publisher of EternityWatch Magazine. Her magazine is focused on holistic health and every issue promotes a holistic approach to health by looking at diet, lifestyle, and your environment. Every issue includes a plant-based recipe for the reader to enjoy.

Her website, Eating4Eternity.org is a wonderful resource for the health-minded that covers topics ranging from square-foot gardening to the living foods.

Look for more great titles from ***The Holistic Health Nurse Series***™

www.holistichealthnurse.com

* * * * *

www.ingramcontent.com/pod-product-compliance
Lightning Source LLC
Chambersburg PA
CBHW071153090426
42736CB00012B/2322